FRESH FLAVOURS OF

india

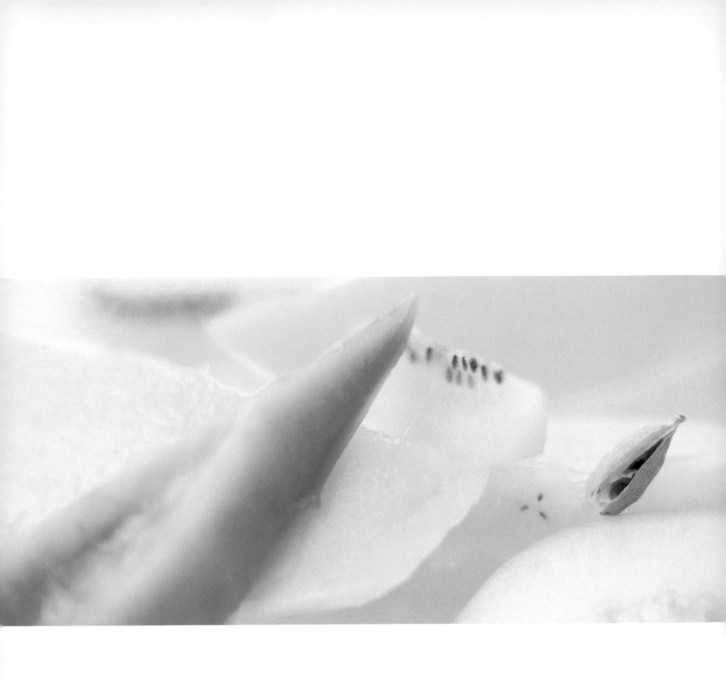

photography by David Loftus

FRESH FLAVOURS OF

india

DAS SREEDHARAN

conran
OCTOPUS

appam

Dedicated to Stoke Newington and its people

First published in 1999 by Conran Octopus Limited
a part of Octopus Publishing Group,
2-4 Heron Quays, London E14 4JP
www.conran-octopus.co.uk

Reprinted in 2000
This paperback edition published in 2002
Reprinted in 2003

Editorial Cookery Consultant: Jenni Muir
Art Editor: Vanessa Courtier
Assistant Editor: Marion Moisy
Design Assistant: Gina Hochstein
Food Stylist: Susie Theodorou
Food Stylist's Assistant: David Morgan
Stylist: Róisín Nield
Photographer's Assistant: Tara Fisher
Production Controller: Sue Sharpless
Commissioning Editor: Stuart Cooper

British Library Cataloguing-in-Publication Data.
A catalogue record for this book is available from
the British Library

ISBN 1 84091 287 1

Colour origination by Sang Choy International,
Singapore. Printed and bound in China.

contents

foreword

In 1986-87, while working in southern India, my colleagues took me to their family homes in rural Kerala. I fell in love with the people, the landscapes, the colours, the aromas, and the astonishing home cooking of this lush and beautiful state.

On my return to Britain I became a restaurant critic and, despite visiting hundreds of Indian restaurants in the capital over many years, I never found anywhere that served proper Keralan food. Then in March 1994 I found Rasa quite by chance, weeks after it opened. I couldn't believe my luck: this was authentic home-style Keralan cooking, par excellence. I kept returning on a weekly basis for more and got to know the charming owner, Das, as we shared a common passion for Kerala.

Eventually I wrote a review of Rasa in *Time Out* magazine and only then did Das rumble me as a restaurant critic, though he treated me no differently. Over the years Das and I have become friends, we have travelled together in Kerala and visited his family, and I have seen his restaurants grow in number and stature.

I haven't written a review of Rasa since that first one, as I could not be impartial. Instead, fellow *Time Out* critics have visited Rasa, and it easily won two successive *Time Out* awards for the Best Vegetarian Meal in London. Many people agree with me that Rasa makes some of the best south Indian dishes you'll find anywhere. I hope this book helps you create the extraordinary flavours of Kerala in your own home.

GUY DIMOND, *Time Out*, 1999

introduction

India is a magical paradise for people who love culture, art, beauty and food. Eating in India is an elaborate function. Religions, regions and time have influenced the cooking history and the style of cooking varies every kilometre, so there is not one clear traditional Indian cuisine. We believe in the golden hands of the chef: great chefs are very respected in the community and hold a high position among the locals. I was brought up in a village of the Nair community in Kerala, a palm-strewn state that lies on the Malabar coast of South India. Known as God's Own Country, it is a tropical region made up almost entirely of inland waterways, coconut groves and spice plantations. Kerala has traded its spices with everyone from Arabs to Chinese to Europeans for thousands of years. Sugatha Kumari, a Keralan poet and ecologist says: "Once there was a time when the whole world was enamoured of the fragrance of Kerala."

I still have very vivid memories of my sister's wedding when I was seven years old. We had the most famous Brahmin chef from Cochin to direct the feast preparations. I was there at 5 o'clock in the morning watching his inspired touch with the spices and his ability to judge quantities without any measuring equipment. At one stage, while I was watching with fascination at the activity before me, he came to me and said: "You may think that it is very difficult to cook, but all you need is passion, care, concentration and — most importantly — love and pride about what you are doing." That was my first lesson in the art of cooking.

My mother's cooking is inspirational, so too my dad's love of food. Eating at our local feasts and temples has given me an amazing experience of Keralan food but, when I began my travels to other parts of India, I realised the depth and beauty of our country's unique cuisine and my appreciation for the different regions grew. How I envied the people in the cities, who had so many different styles of cooking right on their doorstep and were able to sample foods from various regions of India without having to travel. In small villages, one does not find that sort of variety; people eat the same kind of food every day because they do not have such a wide variety of ingredients and knowledge.

On settling in the United Kingdom, like any homesick bachelor, I really missed my Mum's cooking. I searched for typical Indian home cooking in London but soon realized it just did not exist and that the 'Indian food' people were eating was nothing like the cooking I so missed from home. When I began working in restaurants I discovered that many of the chefs working in the Indian restaurant sector were not properly trained and that their knowledge of traditional food was limited. British customers, knowing very little themselves about the cuisine, unquestioningly accepted the food on offer. For my sake, and the sake of everyone who loves Indian food, I began research into something different, something unusual and authentic.

When Rasa opened in 1994 we were immediately recognized for our attention to detail in both food and hospitality. Our passion for cooking can be noticed from the very start of the meal, with our flower-shaped achappams accompanied by our unique array of delicious homemade pickles and chutneys. We have attracted customers from all over the world who have come for this very real experience of Indian food. I expect that in the next decade we will see a lot of restaurants like Rasa opening around the world as a result of people becoming more educated about authentic cuisines.

The style of cooking we have developed at Rasa is one that uses less oil, no artificial colouring and is very judicious with spices, allowing the true flavours of the ingredients to come through. There has been a general trend in recent years towards healthier eating and the enjoyment of fresh, light flavours and this, I believe, is a major attraction of Rasa's style of cooking.

BREAKFAST, LUNCH AND DINNER

Wherever you are in India, from the Nair teashop in Kerala to the Udipi hotels of Madras or the street stalls of Bombay, the smell of freshly fried snacks accompanies you from the moment you step out of your door until you return home. In our village, the teashops open at 5.30am to serve breakfast. People come to read their newspapers and to talk with their friends and neighbours about current affairs and politics. This habit is common in Calcutta as well as Kerala, for these areas have similar intellectual backgrounds and a very high percentage of literacy. Snacks vary from session to session in the teashops; my favourites are the breakfast snacks made of rice flour, such as dosa and appam. Although indigenous to Kerala, these snacks are now like national breakfast dishes and can be found in all Indian cities.

Friends and family constantly talk about my mother's pickles and chutneys after they have moved to far away places. They are indeed a supreme aspect of the meal and, we believe, an essential ingredient to stimulate the taste buds. I could never imagine eating a meal without a chutney or pickle. They allow each diner to combine the components of the meal to suit their own palate.

The menus of most Indian restaurants outside India do not reveal our country's high consumption of vegetarian dishes. We have always eaten more vegetables in our meals than meat, fish or chicken, a deeply rooted combination of religious and economic factors. The majority of Indians are Hindus, who are traditionally vegetarian, and meat has always been much more expensive and less widely available than vegetables. For me, vegetarian cooking has endless attraction. It is all about freshness, aromas and colours. At lunchtimes we tend to eat egg dishes as they are light but have more protein than most of the vegetable dishes.

West Bengal, Goa, Kerala and Mangalore have the best seafood cooking in India and many other things in common, such as the use of coconut and fresh green spices. The Christian influence in the food is also very evident in these places. The fishing communities of India have a special attachment to the Mother Ocean, and this is evident in the lively fish markets. For these people, a meal without fish curry is incomplete. At lunchtime, the fresh aroma of spices and fish cooking fills the air and it is a smell people particularly remember when they are far away from home. With the help of my expert team of chefs at Rasa, we have chosen some seafood delicacies from our own experience and background, based on traditional styles, for inclusion here.

A contemporary Indian cookbook cannot ignore the growing trend for meat eating in most parts of the country. As people have become wealthier, meat has become fashionable and is now a way of life in several areas. Chicken and lamb are the favourites for many Indians, though beef is eaten in some states such as Goa, Kerala and Mangalore. This style of eating is associated more with Christians and Muslims than with Hindus.

In recent years there has been an increase in popularity for beef and other meat dishes, even in the homes of traditional Brahmin people (historically a vegetarian and very religious Hindu caste), the trend is rapidly expanding. My purpose with this book has been to offer a realistic, contemporary reflection of cooking in India rather than a retrospective study, so with the help of the chefs in our restaurants I have chosen a very small number of dishes to demonstrate this aspect of Indian cooking.

Dry dishes or thorans are an inevitable addition to Indian meals, and reveal the healthiness and simplicity of our cooking. We in Kerala always have at least one thoran with each meal. They add beauty and eye-catching contrast to the wet dishes they accompany, but they can also be eaten on their on with bread.

Rice is the staple starch for the majority of Indian people and in South India they cook rice in a vast range of flavours, colours and textures. In North Indian states, however, flat breads are the traditional staples, but today people throughout the country tend to eat a balance of both.

Sweets and puddings are eaten almost every day, although the dishes chosen vary with the occasion and place. Temple puddings have given me lots of sweet memories; pal payasam from the famous Ambalapuzha temple reminds me of devotion and God's liking for auspicious sweets. I am still trying hard to recreate that pudding exactly, but I think that you have to be in the temple itself for that to happen.

This book takes you along the roots of a great cultural change. The history of India can be traced back through its culinary influences and remnants of its many visitors can still be found in the kitchen across India. I hope you feel inspired to try out these dishes: just remember that cooking requires only a little bit of passion, care, concentration and — most importantly — love and pride in what you are doing.

DAS SREEDHARAN London 1999

snacks, pickles & chutneys

ACHAPPAMS

Crunchy achappams are traditionally made using a flower-shaped achappam mould, which can be found in Asian shops. Alternatively, you can make do with a handled biscuit cutter that has been tied to the back of a wooden spoon.

Place the rice flour in a large bowl and add the egg white, coconut milk, black sesame seeds, salt, sugar and cumin. Slowly add 100ml/3½ floz of water while mixing well to give a batter of pouring consistency. Add more water if necessary.

Heat some oil in a deep-fryer, wok or large, heavy saucepan. When the oil is very hot and almost smoking, place the achappam mould into the oil for 10 minutes, until the mould is very hot.

Lift the mould carefully from the oil. Dip it into the batter for 30 seconds, then place it back into the oil without letting it touch the bottom of the pan. The first achappam will take about 5 minutes to cook, the rest a little less.

When the achappam turns light brown, gently shake the mould to remove it. If the achappam is stuck, use a sharp knife to gently lift it off the mould. Leave the achappam in the oil for another 2 minutes until golden. Lift out and drain on kitchen paper.

Repeat the process until all the batter has been used, bearing in mind that it may take you a few tries to master the technique. Serve the achappams cold, with fresh pickles and chutneys.

200g/7oz rice flour
1 egg white
2 tbsp fresh or canned
  coconut milk
1 tsp black sesame seeds
1 tsp salt
½ tsp sugar
¼ tsp cumin seeds
Oil for deep-frying

MAKES 4

CHINNAPPAM

This is a small dry snack, almost like a savoury biscuit, that can be served at the beginning of a meal or with tea in the afternoon.

In a large dry frying pan or wok, toast the rice flour over a moderate heat for 3 to 4 minutes, stirring constantly, until the flour turns golden. Remove from the heat and allow to cool.

Place the shallots, coconut and cumin seeds in a grinder or blender. Add 225ml/8floz of water and process the mixture for 2 to 3 minutes until smooth and combined.

Transfer the toasted rice flour to a large bowl and make a well in the centre. Add the coconut mixture and, using a wooden spoon, work the liquid into the flour until you have a thick, bread-like dough. Add more water if necessary.

Take small amounts of the dough and shape them into balls the size of a large marble. Using your palms, flatten them into small discs and lay them out on a work surface. Continue until all the dough is used.

Heat some oil in a deep-fryer, wok or large, heavy saucepan. When it is hot, fry the chinnappam a few at a time for 2 to 3 minutes or until golden brown. Remove from the oil and drain on kitchen paper. Allow to cool before serving.

400g/14oz rice flour
75g/3oz shallots, peeled
50g/2oz freshly grated or
    desiccated coconut
2 tsp cumin seeds
2 tsp black sesame seeds
Oil for deep-frying
Salt

MAKES 20

BANANA CHIPS

Peel the plantain and slice the flesh very finely. Place in a large bowl and gently mix in the turmeric, curry leaves and some salt to taste.

Heat some oil in a deep-fryer, wok or large, heavy saucepan. Take small amounts of the plantain and fry for 2 to 3 minutes until the chips float to the surface. Use a slotted spoon to remove the chips from the oil and drain on kitchen paper. Continue until all the plantain is used.

Allow the banana chips to cool, then store them in an airtight container until needed. They will stay fresh for up to 1 week.

3 large green plantains
½ tsp turmeric powder
A few curry leaves
Oil for deep-frying
Salt

SERVES 4

GREEN BANANA BHAJIA

Peel and slice the plantain. In a bowl, combine the rice flour, turmeric, chile powder and a little salt. Stir in about 225ml/8floz of water, just enough to make a thick batter.

Heat the oil in a deep-fryer, wok or large, heavy saucepan. Dip the plantain slices in the batter one at a .time and fry until golden brown and crisp. Drain and allow to cool before serving.

1 green plantain
200g/7oz rice flour
½ tsp turmeric powder
½ tsp chile powder
Oil for deep-frying
Salt

SERVES 2

banana boli, banana chips & green banana bhajia

BANANA BOLI

Cut the unpeeled plantain in half lengthways, then cut the halves into 1cm/$\frac{1}{2}$in slices.

In a large bowl, mix together the rice flour, sesame seeds, sugar and turmeric. Slowly stir in 450ml/16floz of water, just enough to give a batter of pouring consistency.

Heat some oil in a deep-fryer, wok or large, heavy saucepan. Peel the plantain slices and place them in the batter. Working one at a time, transfer the coated slices to the oil and fry for 2 to 3 minutes until the batter is cooked.

Remove the boli from the pan and set aside to drain on kitchen paper in a warm place. Serve warm.

2 large ripe plantains
100g/3$\frac{1}{2}$oz rice flour
1 tsp black sesame seeds
1 tsp sugar
$\frac{1}{4}$ tsp turmeric powder
Oil for deep-frying

MAKES 15

CASHEW NUT PAKODAS

Using a pestle and mortar, grind the ginger and green chile to a fine paste. Place in a large bowl with the cashews, rice flour, coriander leaves, black sesame seeds, ghee and a little salt. Add 3 tablespoons of water and stir until the mixture is combined and slightly sticky.

Take small amounts of the mixture and shape them into golfball-sized pieces. Add a little more water if the mixture is not holding together. Gently flatten each ball slightly.

Heat some oil in a deep-fryer, wok or large, heavy saucepan. Take one of the pakodas and drop it in the oil. Cook for 5 minutes, turning once, until it turns golden brown. Remove from the oil and leave to drain on kitchen paper in a warm place. Repeat with the remaining pakodas. Serve warm.

2.5cm/1in cube fresh ginger, peeled and finely chopped
1 green chile, sliced
300g/10$\frac{1}{2}$oz raw cashew nuts
200g/7oz rice flour
2 tbsp roughly chopped coriander leaves
1 tbsp black sesame seeds
1 tbsp ghee
Oil for deep-frying
Salt

MAKES 8

MASALA VADAI

Place the dal in a bowl, cover with water and soak
for 1 hour. Drain thoroughly and grind the dal
in a blender for 2 to 3 minutes — do not grind
too finely, as you want some of the dal to
remain whole to create texture.

Transfer the dal to a large bowl and add the onion,
chiles, ginger, curry leaves and a little salt.
Mix thoroughly to a thick paste.

Heat some oil in a deep-fryer, wok or large, heavy
saucepan. Roll the mixture into golfball-sized
pieces and gently flatten into discs.

Place the vadais in the oil a few at a time and fry
for 5 minutes or until deep golden brown. Remove
and drain on kitchen paper. Serve hot or cold.

400g/14oz chana dal
1 onion, finely chopped
2 green chiles, finely
   chopped
2.5cm/1in cube fresh
   ginger, peeled and
   finely chopped
10 curry leaves, finely
   chopped
Oil for deep-frying
Salt

MAKES 14

KATHRIKKA

Slice the aubergine into 1cm/$\frac{1}{2}$in rounds and soak
in a bowl of water with 2 tablespoons of salt.

Place the remaining ingredients except the oil in a
large bowl and mix well. Stir in 450ml/16floz of
water, or just enough to give a thin batter.
Whisk until thoroughly blended and smooth.

Heat the oil in a deep-fryer, wok or large, heavy
saucepan. Pat dry the aubergine slices and place
them in the batter to coat completely.

Fry the coated aubergine slices one at a time for
2 to 3 minutes until golden. Remove from the oil
and drain on kitchen paper. Serve immediately.

1 medium aubergine
500g/1lb 2oz gram
   (chickpea) flour
2 tbsp chopped coriander
   leaves
1 green chile, chopped
1 tbsp turmeric powder
A pinch of asafoetida
Oil for deep-frying
Salt

MAKES 8

masala vadai & coconut chutney

VEGETABLE CUTLET

In a large pan of boiling salted water, place the beans, carrots, peas, potatoes and the turmeric and simmer for 10 to 15 minutes or until the vegetables are tender. Drain and set aside.

Heat 3 tablespoons of the oil in a large frying pan then add the ginger, mustard seeds, chile powder and curry leaves, and sauté for 2 to 3 minutes. Add the cooked vegetables, stir thoroughly, then add salt to taste. Remove the pan from the heat and set aside to cool.

When the mixture is cool enough to handle, take golfball-sized portions of the mixture and, using wet hands, shape into sausages or patties.

Place the milk in a wide shallow bowl and the breadcrumbs on a tray or plate. Dip each cutlet in the milk, then coat with the breadcrumbs, pressing them on gently.

Rinse and dry the frying pan, then heat another 3 tablespoons of oil in it. Fry the cutlets in batches until crisp and golden brown, turning frequently. Drain on kitchen paper and serve hot.

100g/3$\frac{1}{2}$oz green beans, finely sliced
100g/3$\frac{1}{2}$oz carrots, peeled and finely chopped
100g/3$\frac{1}{2}$oz peas
100g/3$\frac{1}{2}$oz potatoes, peeled and finely chopped
1 tsp turmeric powder
6 tbsp oil
2.5cm/1in cube fresh ginger, peeled and finely sliced
1 tsp mustard seeds
1 tsp chile powder
A few curry leaves, chopped
100ml/3$\frac{1}{2}$floz milk
400g/14oz breadcrumbs
Salt

SERVES 4

DHOKLA

Deepa Kapadia, a friend who produces this light steamed snack whenever I visit, gave me this recipe. Dhoklas are normally made in special steamers but you can use a Chinese-style steamer lined with oiled greaseproof paper.

In separate bowls, soak the rice, chana dal and urad dal in plenty of water for 4 hours.

Drain the pulses and rice separately. Place the chana dal in a blender with 4 teaspoons of sour buttermilk and 4 teaspoons of water. Grind to a coarse, thick batter, then remove and set aside.

Grind the rice and the urad dal together with the rest of the buttermilk and some salt to form a thick batter, adding a little more buttermilk if necessary. Cover both batters with a damp cloth and set aside for 3 hours to ferment.

After fermentation, dissolve the baking soda in the oil, and divide the mixture equally between the batters, stirring until well combined.

In a frying pan, heat 1 tablespoon of the ghee and fry the coconut, green chiles and garlic for 2 minutes. Pour over the chana dal batter, add the coriander leaves and mix thoroughly.

Heat the rest of the ghee in the frying pan and add the ginger, dried chiles, curry leaves, mustard and cumin seeds. Cook for 2 to 3 minutes, then pour over the rice batter and stir well.

Cut a few slits in some greaseproof paper and oil it lightly. Use this to line a steamer and set it over simmering water. Pour a little chana dal batter onto the paper and carefully cover with the same quantity of rice batter. Cover and cook for 10 to 15 minutes until firm. Remove and cut into diamond shapes, then repeat with the rest of the batter. Serve hot, with coconut chutney.

a200g/7oz long-grain rice
200g/7oz chana dal
75g/3oz urad dal
100ml/3$\frac{1}{2}$ floz sour buttermilk
$\frac{1}{2}$ tsp baking soda
2 tbsp vegetable oil, plus extra for greasing
2 tbsp ghee
200g/7oz freshly grated or desiccated coconut
4 green chiles, finely chopped
4 cloves garlic, chopped
2 tsp chopped coriander leaves
2.5cm/1in cube fresh ginger, peeled and chopped
2 dried red chiles, chopped
2 tsp chopped curry leaves
1 tsp mustard seeds
1 tsp cumin seeds
Salt

SERVES 4

SEMOLINA UPPUMA

Heat a large, heavy saucepan over a medium heat and toast the semolina for 5 minutes, stirring continuously, until the grains turn golden. Remove from the heat and set aside.

In another heavy saucepan, heat the ghee or oil. When hot, add the mustard seeds, cumin, urad dal, chana dal, red chile and curry leaves. As the mustard seeds begin to pop, add the chopped onions, green chiles, ginger, turmeric and some salt. Sauté the mixture over a medium heat for 5 minutes, stirring frequently.

Add 700ml/1 pint 4floz of water to the pan, cover and simmer for 5 minutes. Slowly add the toasted semolina, stirring continuously to avoid lumps forming. Cook uncovered over a low heat until all the water has been absorbed. Remove the pan from the heat and mix in the lemon juice.

To serve, pour the mixture into several small moulds such as pudding basins, cups or bowls. Press well into the containers, then turn them over onto serving plates. Gently remove the moulds and serve hot.

400g/14oz coarse semolina
3 tbsp ghee or oil
1 tsp mustard seeds
1 tsp cumin seeds
1 tsp urad dal
1 tsp chana dal
1 dried red chile
A few curry leaves
2 medium onions, finely chopped
2 green chiles, finely sliced
2.5cm/1in cube fresh ginger, peeled and finely chopped
$1/2$ tsp turmeric powder
Juice of 1 lemon
Salt

SERVES 4

SUNDAL

Chickpeas are an ingredient typically associated with the cooking of northern India, but this simple Tamil Nadu recipe is one of the few ways in which they are served in the south. The Tamils tend to have chickpeas in stock because they eat them for breakfast; they then make this snack, which would be served with coffee, using the leftovers. The fresh flavour of coconut provides a delicious contrast to the chickpeas.

If using dried chickpeas, place them in a large bowl, cover generously with water and soak for 7 to 8 hours. When ready to cook, drain the chickpeas and place them in a large saucepan. Cover with 700ml/1 pint 4floz of water, bring to the boil and simmer the chickpeas gently for 35 to 45 minutes, until they are well cooked. If using canned chickpeas, rinse them and cook in a small amount of water for about 15 minutes, then drain and set aside.

Heat the oil in a large frying pan. When hot, add the red chile, mustard seeds and urad dal. As the mustard seeds begin to pop, add the cooked chickpeas, coconut, green chile and a little salt. Mix thoroughly, remove from the heat and stir in the lemon juice. Serve hot or cold.

300g/10½ oz dried chickpeas, or 400g/14oz canned chickpeas
2 tsp oil
1 fresh red chile, halved
1 tsp mustard seeds
1 tsp urad dal
3 tbsp freshly grated or desiccated coconut
1 green chile, finely chopped
Juice of 1 lemon
Salt

SERVES 2

snacks, pickles & chutneys 2 9

DOSA MASALA

This simple but exquisite mixture of potatoes cooked with ginger, onion and curry leaves can be eaten as a side dish or with poories but I believe it is best served the traditional way, as a stuffing for dosas (pancakes), with coconut chutney on the side.

Place the whole, unpeeled potatoes in a large saucepan and cover them with water. Bring to the boil and simmer until the potatoes are cooked but firm.

Meanwhile, heat the oil in a large frying pan over a high heat. Add the mustard seeds and, as they begin to pop, add the curry leaves and chiles and cook for 30 seconds. Add the onions, stir well and cook over a medium heat for 10 minutes or until the onions are well browned.

When the potatoes are cooked, remove from the heat and drain. Set aside until they are cool enough to handle. Peel the potatoes, then return them to the saucepan and mash roughly.

When the onions are brown, add the tomato, ginger, turmeric and salt. Stir and cook for 5 minutes over a low heat.

Add the mashed potatoes to the onion mixture and stir thoroughly. Cook for another 3 to 4 minutes then remove from the heat.

Make the dosas according to the recipe on page 55, placing the potato mixture on the uncooked side of the pancakes. Fold and serve.

700g/1lb 8oz potatoes
3 tbsp oil
1 tsp mustard seeds
About 20 curry leaves
2 green chiles, finely sliced
200g/7oz onions, finely sliced
1 medium tomato, chopped
1cm/½ in cube fresh ginger, peeled and finely sliced
½ tsp turmeric powder
Salt
1 quantity dosa recipe (see page 55)

MAKES 10

NAIR DOSA

My mother taught me this variation of the dosa masala last time I was in Kerala. Nair dosa is often served for breakfast on festival days, as the colours help to brighten the morning.

In a large saucepan of salted water, place the potatoes, bring to the boil and simmer for 8 to 10 minutes, until the potatoes are cooked but firm. Add the cubed carrots to the pan after about 3 minutes. In a separate pan of water, boil the peas until just tender. When cooked, drain the potatoes, carrots and peas.

In a large frying pan, heat the oil over a high heat. Add the mustard seeds and, as they begin to pop, add the chiles and curry leaves and cook for 30 seconds. Add the onions and stir well. Lower the heat to medium and cook for 10 minutes or until the onions are well browned.

Stir in the tomato, ginger, garam masala and turmeric and add salt to taste. Cook the mixture for 5 minutes over a low heat.

Add the potatoes, carrots, peas and beetroot and mix thoroughly. Cook for another 3 to 4 minutes then remove from the heat.

Make 12 small dosas according to the recipe on page 55, placing the beetroot mixture on the uncooked side of the pancakes. Fold and serve.

400g/14oz potatoes, peeled and cubed
150g/5oz carrots, cubed
100g/3½ oz green peas
3 tbsp oil
1 tsp mustard seeds
2 green chiles, finely sliced
About 20 curry leaves
200g/7oz onions, finely sliced
1 medium tomato, chopped
1cm/½ in cube fresh ginger, peeled and finely sliced
½ tsp garam masala
½ tsp turmeric powder
100g/3½ oz cooked beetroot (not pickled), cubed
1 quantity dosa recipe (see page 55)
Salt

MAKES 12

VEGETABLE SAMOSAS

If you do not want to use all of the samosas at once you can store any that are uncooked in the freezer for up to 1 month. To prepare them, remove them from the freezer, allow to defrost and then fry them as needed.

Heat the 3 tablespoons of oil in a large frying pan. Add the mustard seeds and, as they begin to pop, add the onions and curry leaves and cook for 5 minutes over a medium heat until the onions are soft.

Mix in the turmeric, chile powder, garam masala and some salt, then add the vegetables and stir well. Cover and cook for 15 to 20 minutes, stirring frequently, until the vegetables are tender. Remove the pan from the heat and set aside to cool.

Fold each sheet of pastry in half lengthways to give two layers and cut into strips measuring about 7.5cm/3in x 30cm/12in.

Place a tablespoon of the vegetable mixture in the middle at the end of a pastry strip. Fold a corner of the pastry over the mixture to form a triangle and continue folding in alternate directions to give a triangular parcel. Repeat with the remaining pastry and filling.

Heat the oil for deep-frying in a deep-fryer, wok or large, heavy saucepan. When the oil is very hot, gently place the samosas, one at a time, in the oil and fry for 2 to 3 minutes or until golden brown. Remove each cooked samosa and drain on kitchen paper, then serve hot or cold.

3 tbsp oil, plus extra for deep-frying
1 tsp mustard seeds
2 medium onions, finely sliced
A few curry leaves
1/2 tsp turmeric powder
1/4 tsp chile powder
1/4 tsp garam masala
2 potatoes, diced
1 carrot, diced
150g/5oz green beans, diced
150g/5oz peas
250g/9oz ready-made samosa pastry or filo pastry, defrosted if frozen
Salt

MAKES 20

SUKIAN

This sweet snack made from green mung beans and jaggery is a speciality served in Keralan teashops during the afternoon. The soft, light patty goes well with any cold drink, tea or coffee.

Put a pan of salted water on to boil. Wash the mung beans and place them in the boiling water, then simmer for 20 to 25 minutes or until the beans are tender and well cooked. Drain and set aside.

Place the jaggery or brown sugar in a bowl and, with the back of a wooden spoon or a fork, break it up to give a coarse powder (you can also grind it in a spice mill). Add the coconut and mix well, then stir in the cooked mung beans.

In another bowl, place the flour and make a well in the centre. Slowly add 450ml/16floz of water, mixing with a wooden spoon to give a batter of pouring consistency.

Heat some oil in a deep-fryer, wok or large, heavy saucepan. When hot, take a small ball of the bean mixture and dip it in the batter. Gently drop it in the oil and cook for 2 to 3 minutes, or until golden brown. Remove the sukian from the oil and drain on kitchen paper. Repeat with the rest of the mixture and serve hot.

600g/1lb 5oz green mung beans
100g/3$\frac{1}{2}$oz jaggery or brown sugar
150g/5oz freshly grated or desiccated coconut
200g/7oz plain flour
Oil for deep-frying
Salt

MAKES 20

UNDAN PORI

A familiar sight in Keralan teashops, where they are displayed in glass boxes, these sweet, deep-fried snacks are inexpensive and therefore a particular favourite with children, who buy them with their pocket money and throw them at each other. Of course, they like to eat them too.

Combine all the ingredients except the oil in a large bowl and make a well in the centre. Slowly add 200ml/7floz of water, mixing with a wooden spoon to give a thick, sticky batter. Cover the bowl with a damp cloth and leave the mixture to stand for 20 minutes.

Heat some oil in a deep-fryer, wok or large, heavy saucepan. Using wet hands, take portions of the batter and roll them into balls about the size of a golfball.

Working in batches, drop a few balls gently into the oil and cook for 5 minutes, or until they turn golden brown and float to the top of the oil. Remove from the oil and drain on kitchen paper. Repeat with the rest of the balls. Serve hot with tea or coffee.

500g/1lb 4oz plain flour
2 bananas, mashed
100g/3½ oz jaggery or
  brown sugar, crumbled
1 tsp jeera cumin seeds
½ tsp baking soda
Oil for deep-frying

MAKES 20

CORIANDER CHUTNEY

Many people will recognise this fresh chutney: it is the one most Indian restaurants tend to make themselves. Traditionally we would not serve it with poppadoms, but alongside a selection of curries.

Place all the ingredients in a blender and process for 2 to 3 minutes or until smooth.

Transfer the mixture to an airtight container or screw-top jar and store in the refrigerator for up to 4 days.

200ml/7floz plain yogurt
100g/3½oz fresh
    coriander leaves
100g/3½oz freshly
    grated or desiccated
    coconut
5 garlic cloves, peeled
2 green chiles
Salt

SERVES 4

COCONUT CHUTNEY

In a grinder or blender, process the coconut, green chiles, ginger and a little salt to a fine paste. Transfer the mixture to a bowl, add the yogurt, stir well and set aside.

In a small frying pan, heat the oil over a medium heat and, when hot, add the mustard seeds and curry leaves. As the mustard seeds begin to pop, add the coconut paste, then lower the heat and cook for 5 minutes, stirring occasionally.

Remove from the heat and leave the mixture to cool before serving. This chutney can be stored in the fridge for 2 days if kept in an airtight container or screw-top jar.

100g/3½oz freshly
    grated or desiccated
    coconut
2 green chiles
2.5cm/1in cube fresh
    ginger, peeled and
    sliced
3 tbsp yogurt
2 tbsp oil
1 tsp mustard seeds
10 curry leaves
Salt

SERVES 4

LIME PICKLE

Lime pickle is typical of the Namboothiri homes in Kerala. A very popular way to enjoy it is to add a dash to payasam (pudding), at the end of the meal, for a final touch of spiciness, but I only recommend this to the very brave.

In a large pan, heat 1 tablespoon of the oil over a medium heat. Add the asafoetida, fenugreek seeds and dried chiles and cook for 2 minutes, stirring continuously. Remove from the heat and set aside to cool. Transfer the mixture to a spice mill and grind until very fine.

Heat the remaining 3 tablespoons of oil in the same pan, then add the whole limes. Cook them over a medium heat for 15 minutes, turning frequently, until the skins turn deep brown all over. Remove from the heat and set aside to cool.

When the limes are cool enough to handle, wipe the oil from the skins with kitchen paper. Cut the limes into quarters and place in a bowl. Add the spice mixture and salt and mix thoroughly until the limes are covered with spices.

Allow the limes to cool completely, then place in a screw-top jar and store in a cool, dry place for a week before using, gently shaking the jar once a day to distribute the juices. The pickle will keep for up to 2 months.

4 tbsp oil
1 tsp asafoetida
1 tsp fenugreek seeds
4 dried red chiles
10 limes
5-6 tsp salt

MAKES 1 JAR

LEMON PICKLE

Wash the lemon thoroughly and cut it into very fine pieces, removing the seeds. Place the chopped lemon in a bowl.

Heat the oil in a large frying pan. Add the mustard seeds and, as they begin to pop, add the curry leaves and urad dal, if using. When the dal begins to brown, lower the heat and add the chile powder, then the vinegar. Slowly stir the lemon into the mixture until thoroughly blended.

Add the asafoetida, stir well, then remove the pan from the heat and set aside to cool. Transfer the lemon pickle to a screw-top jar and store in the fridge, where it will keep for up to 1 week.

1 medium lemon
1 tbsp oil
1 tsp mustard seeds
A few curry leaves
* (optional)*
1 tsp urad dal (optional)
1 tsp chile powder
2 tbsp vinegar
A small pinch of
* asafoetida*
Salt

SERVES 4

MANGO PICKLE

This pickle tastes best when left to mature for a week before eating, but the result is well worth the wait.

Place the fenugreek in a small frying pan and toast gently over a very low heat, stirring constantly, for 5 minutes or until golden brown. Finely grind using a pestle and mortar and set aside.

Place the mango in a large bowl. Mix in the salt, chile powder, asafoetida and ground fenugreek.

Heat the oil in a frying pan. Add the mustard seeds and, as they begin to pop, add the curry leaves and dried chiles. Fry over a medium heat for 1 minute, then pour the contents of the pan over the mango. Mix well and set aside to cool.

When cool, transfer to a screw-top jar and store in the refrigerator for up to 1 month. Leave the pickle to mature for 1 week before use.

1 tsp fenugreek seeds
200g/7oz green mangoes,
* diced*
1 tbsp salt
2 tsp chile powder
1 tsp asafoetida
2 tbsp oil
1 tsp mustard seeds
10 curry leaves
4 dried red chiles

MAKES 1 JAR

GOOSEBERRY PICKLE

Clean and dry the gooseberries and place in a bowl. Crush the fruit roughly. Remove and discard the seeds and set the gooseberries aside.

Place the dried chiles and fenugreek seeds in a large frying pan and toast for 2 to 3 minutes, stirring. Transfer to a spice mill, grind to a fine powder and set aside.

Heat the oil in the frying pan. Add the mustard seeds and, as they being to pop, stir in the turmeric. Add the crushed gooseberries, mix well and cook for 15 minutes over a low heat.

Remove the pan from the heat and set aside to cool. Add the ground chiles and fenugreek, asafoetida and a little salt to the fruit and mix well. Store the mixture in a screw-top jar in the fridge for up to 1 month.

200g/7oz gooseberries, trimmed
4 dried red chiles
1 tsp fenugreek seeds
4 tbsp oil
1 tsp mustard seeds
1 tsp turmeric powder
A pinch of asafoetida
Salt

MAKES 1 JAR

GARLIC PICKLE

Heat the oil in a large non-stick frying pan. Add the fenugreek seeds, cook until lightly browned, then add the garlic and stir-fry for 5 minutes.

Stir in the chile powder, turmeric and a little salt, then pour in the vinegar. Cook over a low heat until most of the liquid has evaporated and the garlic is tender and well cooked.

Leave the mixture to cool then transfer it to a screw-top jar. The pickle will keep in the fridge for up to 2 weeks.

1 tbsp oil
A few fenugreek seeds
100g/3$\frac{1}{2}$ oz garlic cloves, thickly sliced
$\frac{1}{2}$ tsp chile powder
$\frac{1}{4}$ tsp turmeric powder
200ml/7floz vinegar
1 tsp white sugar
Salt

MAKES 1 JAR

breads, dosas & rice

pilau rice & lemon rice

PILAU RICE

Stirring a tablespoon of ghee into the cooked rice just before serving gives this dish the authentic flavour of India.

Wash the rice thoroughly and set aside to drain. In a small saucepan, heat the milk to just below scalding point and add the saffron strands. Stir, then remove from the heat and set aside to infuse.

Heat 3 tablespoons of oil in a small frying pan and add half the onion. Cook over a medium heat until the onion is well browned and crisp, then remove and drain on kitchen paper. Set aside until serving.

In a large saucepan, heat 5 tablespoons of oil and add the cashews, cardamon, cloves, peppercorns, bay leaves and cinnamon. Cook, stirring, over a medium heat for 2 minutes until fragrant.

Add the remaining raw onion to the spices and cook, stirring, until the onion is lightly browned. Stir in the rice and 1 litre/1 pint 15 floz of water. Add a little salt, then lower the heat, cover and cook for about 20 minutes or until the rice is tender but firm. If the rice becomes too dry during cooking, add some more water.

Drain the rice to remove any excess water then return it to the saucepan and stir in the saffron milk and the ghee, if using. Garnish with the reserved crispy onions and serve hot.

250g/9oz basmati rice
5 tbsp milk
5 saffron threads
8 tbsp oil
1 large onion, finely
  chopped
25g/1oz raw cashew nuts
5 cardamon pods
5 cloves
5 black peppercorns
2 bay leaves
1 cinnamon stick
1 tbsp ghee (optional)
Salt

SERVES 4

LEMON RICE

Light and tangy, with the refreshing flavour of lemon juice, this subtle rice dish accompanies Keralan food very well. In India, it tends to be made on special occasions such as celebrations and when entertaining guests.

Wash the rice in cold water and place it in a large, heavy saucepan. Add 700ml/1 pint 4 floz of fresh water, the turmeric powder and a little salt. Stir well, bring to the boil and simmer for 20 minutes or until the rice is cooked.

Drain the rice thoroughly, return it to the saucepan and add the lemon juice, mixing well. Set aside in a warm place.

In a small frying pan, heat the oil over a medium heat. Add the mustard seeds and, as they begin to pop, add the urad dal and curry leaves. Stir and cook for 2 to 3 minutes, then pour the contents of the frying pan over the lemon rice.

Transfer to a serving dish and garnish with the lemon zest, coriander leaves and extra curry leaves.

200g/7oz long-grain or basmati rice
1/2 tsp turmeric powder
Juice of 1/2 lemon
2 tbsp oil
1 tbsp mustard seeds
1 tsp urad dal
A few curry leaves, plus extra to garnish
1 tbsp finely grated lemon zest
A few coriander leaves
Salt

SERVES 4

COCONUT RICE

Wash the rice in cold water and place it in a large pot. Add 1 litre/1 pint 15floz of water and a little salt. Bring to the boil and simmer for about 20 minutes, or until the rice is just soft. Drain the excess water from the rice and set aside.

Heat the oil in a small saucepan, then add the mustard seeds, urad dal and curry leaves and cook until the dal is brown. Stir in the coconut and cook for another 3 to 4 minutes, then remove from the heat.

Combine the coconut mixture and rice in a serving bowl and garnish with the extra curry leaves.

250g/9oz basmati rice
1 tbsp oil
1 tsp mustard seeds
1 tsp urad dal
A few curry leaves, plus extra to garnish
50g/2oz freshly grated or desiccated coconut
Salt

SERVES 4

THAKKALI CHORU

Choru is the Malayalam word for rice and thakkali means tomato. In Kerala, tomato rice is made in many ways but I think this recipe, which comes from my sister Padmini, is very special. She is typical of many female cooks in that part of India in that she likes to experiment in the kitchen, developing new recipes and modernizing traditional dishes.

Wash the rice and set aside to drain. In a large saucepan, heat the oil over a medium heat and add the cashews, bay leaves, cinnamon, mustard seeds and curry leaves. Cook, stirring, for 2 to 3 minutes or until fragrant.

Add the onion and cook for 10 minutes or until the onion is well browned. Mix in the tomato, tomato paste, chile powder and turmeric powder. Cover and cook for 20 minutes over a very low heat, stirring occasionally, until a thick sauce forms.

Meanwhile, in a large pan of boiling salted water, cook the rice for 20 minutes or until tender. Drain and refresh under cold running water, then set aside to drain thoroughly.

When the tomato sauce is cooked, add the cooked rice, some of the chopped coriander and mint leaves and mix well. Transfer to a serving dish, garnish with the remaining chopped herbs and serve.

250g/9oz long-grain rice
2 tbsp oil
10 raw cashew nuts
2 bay leaves
1 cinnamon stick
1 tsp mustard seeds
A few curry leaves
1 onion, finely sliced
200g/7oz tomato, finely chopped
2 tbsp tomato paste
1 tsp chile powder
1 tsp turmeric powder
A few coriander leaves, finely chopped
A few mint leaves, finely chopped
Salt

SERVES 4

TAMARIND RICE

Tamarind rice is a traditional speciality of the high caste Brahmin people of Tamil Nadu and they would typically enjoy this dish several times a week. Using tamarind in this way is very unusual, except in that part of India, but it is a delicious combination that is highly popular in our restaurants. I like to serve it alongside moru kachiathu with green banana and mango.

In a small saucepan, bring 100ml/3½floz of water to the boil, then add the tamarind and simmer for 20 minutes or until the water thickens, stirring occasionally. Remove from the heat and sieve the mixture into a bowl. Set aside.

In a large saucepan, bring 500ml/18floz of water to the boil. Add the rice and a little salt to taste and cook for 20 to 25 minutes, or until the rice is tender. Drain and set aside.

Rinse out the saucepan, add the oil and place over a medium heat. Add the mustard seeds and, as they begin to pop, add the onion, peanuts, chana dal or lentils, curry leaves, dried chiles and fenugreek seeds. Cook, stirring frequently, until the onions are soft and golden.

Add the asafoetida, chile powder, coriander, turmeric and some salt. Cook over a medium heat, stirring, for 2 to 3 minutes. Pour in the tamarind water, mix well and cook for 15 minutes, or until thick.

Add the rice, stir to combine and remove the pan from the heat. Transfer the rice to a serving dish and garnish with the extra curry leaves.

50g/2oz tamarind pulp
250g/9oz long-grain rice
2 tbsp oil
1 tsp mustard seeds
1 onion, finely chopped
20g/¾oz raw peanuts
1 tbsp chana dal or yellow lentils
10 curry leaves, plus extra to garnish
3 dried red chiles
1 tsp fenugreek seeds
1 tsp asafoetida
1 tsp chile powder
1 tsp ground coriander
1 tsp turmeric powder
Salt

SERVES 4

ARI PATHIRI

Ari pathiri is a Muslim speciality bread particularly associated with the Ramzan or Ramadan festival. It is to the Malabar region what the chapati is to North India, and is usually eaten with meat dishes such as beef chile, but it is also good with vegetable curries.

Place the rice flour in a large dry frying pan, and toast over a medium heat for 5 minutes or until the flour turns golden brown, stirring constantly.

Place the coconut and cumin seeds in a grinder and process for 2 to 3 minutes, or until finely ground.

Combine the rice flour, coconut mixture and a little salt in a large bowl. Make a well in the centre and gradually stir in about 450ml/16floz of water to make a soft dough.

With floured hands, knead the dough and shape it into small balls. Roll out the balls on a surface dusted with rice flour and leave to rest for 10 minutes.

Heat a large frying pan and coat the base of the pan with oil. Place one disc of dough in the pan and cook for 2 to 3 minutes until golden brown. Turn and repeat on the other side. Cook the remaining discs the same way, then serve hot.

300g/10½oz rice flour
50g/2oz freshly grated
   or desiccated coconut
1 tsp cumin seeds
Oil for frying
Salt

SERVES 4

UTHAPPAM

A very typical breakfast or afternoon dish, uthappam is what I would call a Keralan version of pizza, but made without cheese. It is best cooked on an iron griddle if you have one — alternatively, use a large, heavy frying pan.

In a large bowl, soak the rice overnight or for at least 8 hours in 700ml/1 pint 4floz of water. In a separate bowl, soak the urad dal and fenugreek seeds in about 225ml/8floz of water.

Drain the rice and dal, keeping them separate. Place the rice in a blender and process for a few minutes, slowly adding 120ml/4floz of water to give a smooth paste. Remove the paste from the blender and place in a very large bowl.

Rinse out the blender and place the urad dal in it. Process for 5 minutes, slowly adding 4 tablespoons of water. Add the dal mixture to the rice paste and mix well. Stir in a little salt and cover with a damp cloth. Leave to ferment for 12 hours, until the batter has increased in volume and become a mass of small bubbles. Add a little water to give a thick pouring consistency.

Heat a griddle or large, heavy frying pan until very hot and have the vegetables ready to add to the pancakes. Lightly grease the pan with oil.

Pour a ladle of batter onto the surface and spread it out slightly with a spoon so it is like a Scotch pancake. Top with some of the tomato, onion, green chile and coriander. Cook for about 2 minutes or until the bottom is golden brown.

Brush the edges of the pancake with oil and carefully turn it over using an egg slice or spatula. Cook for another 2 to 3 minutes until the other side is cooked and the onion and tomato brown slightly. Set aside in a warm place while you cook the remaining uthappam. Serve with coconut chutney.

For the batter:
300g/10½oz long-grain
  rice
75g/3oz urad dal
½ tsp fenugreek seeds
Oil for frying
Salt

For the topping:
4 tomatoes, thickly sliced
1 medium onion, finely
  sliced or chopped
2 green chiles, finely
  sliced
2 tbsp fresh coriander
  leaves

MAKES 8

UZHUNNAPPAM

Place the urad dal in a small frying pan and toast over a medium heat until the dal turns golden brown. Transfer to a spice mill and grind to a fine powder. Place the powder in a large bowl and set aside.

Grind the shallots, garlic and cumin seeds coarsely and transfer the mixture to the bowl. Add the ground rice and coconut and slowly stir in 450ml/16floz of water, or just enough to give a thick batter.

Heat 1 teaspoon of oil in a large frying pan over a medium heat. Pour a ladle of batter into the pan and swirl it round to cover the base. Cook until crisp and golden underneath, about 4 to 5 minutes. Turn over carefully and cook for another 3 to 4 minutes. Remove from the pan and serve immediately. Repeat with the remaining batter.

50g/2oz urad dal
10 shallots, finely chopped
3 cloves garlic
1 tsp cumin seeds
200g/7oz ground rice
50g/2oz freshly grated or
  desiccated coconut
Oil for frying
Salt

MAKES 8

POORIES

Place the flour, oil and a pinch of salt in a bowl. Slowly add about 200ml/7floz of water and mix to a smooth dough. Leave to stand for 10 minutes.

Knead the dough on a floured work surface for about 3 minutes. Take golfball-sized pieces of the dough and roll them out as thinly as possible, turning the poori to give an even, round shape.

Heat the oil in a deep-fryer, wok or large, heavy saucepan, and heat a dry frying pan to toast the poori. When the oil is very hot, place a poori in the frying pan and toast for 30 seconds each side.

Transfer the toasted poori to the oil and fry for 2 to 3 minutes, turning constantly to help it puff up. Remove from the pan and drain on kitchen paper. Repeat with the remaining poories.

400g/14oz plain flour
1 tbsp oil
Oil for deep-frying
Salt

MAKES 12

APPAM

Traditionally cooked in a quad — like a small lidded wok — these lacy rice pancakes are made to order in view of customers in our restaurants. Appams are a Christian speciality, traditionally served at Easter.

Wash the rice in some cold water, then transfer to a bowl and cover with 500ml/18floz of fresh water. Leave the rice to soak for 1 hour, then drain, reserving 225ml/8floz of the water.

Transfer the rice and reserved water to a grinder. Add the coconut and grind finely, then set aside.

Place 5 teaspoons of lukewarm water in a small bowl. Add the sugar, stir to dissolve, then add the yeast. Cover the bowl with plastic wrap and set aside.

Place the semolina in a saucepan and add 150ml/5floz of water. Set over a medium heat and cook for about 15 minutes, stirring occasionally, until thick. Remove from the heat.

In a large bowl, place the ground rice, yeast mixture and cooked semolina. Stir well and cover with a damp cloth. Leave to ferment for at least 4 hours, or until the mixture is slightly bubbly and has doubled in volume (which may take longer in cold weather).

Add the salt to the batter and stir well, without knocking the air out of the mixture.

Lightly grease a quad or large non-stick frying pan and place over a medium heat. Add a ladle of the appam mixture and spread it thinly over the base of the pan as you would a crêpe. Cover and cook for 2 to 3 minutes, until the base is golden and crisp and the top surface is soft and pale.

Use an egg slice or spatula to remove the appam from the pan, then repeat with the remaining mixture. Serve as soon as possible.

250g/9oz basmati rice
125g/4$\frac{1}{2}$oz freshly grated
    or desiccated coconut
1 tsp sugar
1 tsp dried yeast
75g/3oz semolina
1 tsp salt
Oil for frying

DOSAS

South India's most famous dish, and one that can now be found anywhere in the country, dosas are remarkably easy to make. This recipe is for the basic dosa, which can be filled with many varieties of stuffing but is most usually served with a mixture of potato and ginger (see page 30). Dosas are also served plain with coconut chutney as a breakfast dish.

In a large bowl, soak the rice for at least 8 hours in 700ml/1 pint 4 floz of water. At the same time, in a separate bowl, soak the urad dal and fenugreek.

Drain the rice and dal, keeping them separate. Place the rice in a blender and grind for 2 to 3 minutes, slowly adding 125ml/4floz of water to give a smooth paste. Transfer the paste to a large bowl.

Rinse out the blender, then grind the urad dal for 5 minutes, slowly adding 4 tablespoons of water to make a paste. Add the dal paste to the bowl of rice paste and mix well. Stir in some salt, then cover the bowl with a damp cloth. Leave to ferment for 12 hours, during which time the batter will increase in volume and become a mass of small bubbles.

When ready to cook, add a little bit of water so that the batter is of a thick pouring consistency.

Heat an iron griddle or large, heavy frying pan until very hot. Lightly grease the pan with oil, then pour on a ladle of batter and use the bottom of the ladle to quickly spread the batter out thinly using a spiral motion. Brush the edges of the dosa with oil and cook for 2 to 3 minutes until the bottom of the dosa is crisp and golden.

If you are using a filling, add it to the uncooked side of the dosa, fold and serve. Otherwise, turn the dosa carefully using an egg slice or spatula and cook for 2 to 3 minutes on the other side until golden. Serve immediately or the dosa will become limp and soggy. Repeat with the remaining batter.

295g/10½ oz long-grain rice
75g/3oz urad dal
½ tsp fenugreek seeds
Oil for frying
Salt

MAKES 12

WHEAT DOSA

Sift the plain and rice flours into a large bowl. Make
a well in the centre and slowly stir in 225ml/8floz
of water, just enough to give a smooth batter of
pouring consistency. Add the coconut, chiles, ginger
and a little salt and mix well.

Heat a griddle or large, heavy frying pan. When hot,
rub the surface with a little oil and pour a ladle
of batter onto the griddle. Spread out the batter
evenly, using the ladle base in a spiral motion.

Brush the top of the dosa with some oil and cook for
3 to 5 minutes over a medium heat until golden
brown. Turn and cook for a further 2 to 3 minutes.
Remove from the heat and serve hot. Repeat with the
remaining batter.

275g/10oz plain flour
2 tbsp rice flour
3 tbsp freshly grated or
*   desiccated coconut*
2 green chiles, finely
*   chopped*
2.5cm/1in cube fresh
*   ginger, peeled and*
*   finely chopped*
Oil for frying
Salt

MAKES 6

RAVA DOSA

Place the semolina and rice flour in a large bowl.
Slowly pour in 700ml/1 pint 4floz of water, mixing
well, then stir in the coconut, red onion, green
chiles, ginger, cumin seeds, curry leaves
and a little salt.

Heat a griddle or large frying pan. Rub it with a
little oil, then pour on a ladle of batter, letting
it spread out. Cook for 2 to 3 minutes, or until
crisp and brown underneath.

Brush the top of the dosa with some oil and turn it
over. Cook for another 2 minutes, then remove the
dosa from the heat and set aside in a warm place.
Repeat with the remaining batter, stirring it well
before you add it to the pan. Serve hot.

160g/5$\frac{1}{2}$oz semolina
80g/3oz rice flour
50g/2oz desiccated coconut
1 red onion, finely
*   chopped*
2 green chiles, finely
*   sliced*
2.5cm/1in cube fresh
*   ginger, peeled and*
*   sliced*
1 tsp cumin seeds
A few curry leaves,
*   chopped*
Oil for frying
Salt

MAKES 8

KAL DOSA

In a large bowl, soak the rice overnight or for at
least 8 hours in twice its amount of water. At the
same time, in a separate bowl, soak the urad dal
and fenugreek seeds in water. When ready to proceed,
drain the rice and dal, keeping them separate.

Place the rice in a blender and grind it for 2 to
3 minutes, slowly adding 125ml/4floz of water to
give a smooth paste. Remove the paste from the
blender and place in a large bowl.

Rinse out the blender, then grind the urad dal for
5 minutes, gradually adding 4 tablespoons of water.
Add the dal paste and a little salt to the bowl of
rice paste and mix well. Cover with a damp cloth
and leave to ferment for 12 hours, during which
time the batter will increase in volume and become
a mass of small bubbles.

When ready to cook, add a little bit of water to give
the batter a thick pouring consistency, then stir in
the chopped vegetables and herbs.

Heat an iron griddle or large, heavy frying pan until
very hot. Lightly grease the pan with oil and pour
on a ladle of batter, using the bottom of the ladle
to quickly spread the batter out to the size and
thickness of a Scotch pancake. Brush the edges of
the dosa with oil and cook for 2 to 3 minutes until
the base is crisp and golden.

Using an egg slice or spatula, carefully turn the dosa
over. Cook for 2 to 3 minutes on the other side, or
until golden. Remove from the pan and serve hot.
Repeat with the remaining batter.

300g/10½ oz long-grain
rice
75g/3oz urad dal
½ tsp fenugreek seeds
1 onion, finely chopped
1 tomato, finely chopped
4 green chiles, finely
sliced
A few coriander leaves,
chopped
Oil for frying
Salt

MAKES 12

dry dishes & side dishes

BLACK-EYED BEAN THORAN

Thorans are an essential part of Keralan meals, especially at feasts. They are dry dishes of vegetables stir-fried with onion, coconut and curry leaves. Many different vegetables can be used, as long as they stay firm when cooked, so spinach, for example, is not a good choice. This bean version can be served hot or cold, as a side dish or salad. It is always best to cook the beans yourself, but if you are pushed for time or simply feeling a little lazy, canned beans can be used — if so, wash them well under cold water to remove all the liquor or it will spoil the taste of the finished dish.

Soak the dried beans in cold water for about 6 hours. When ready to cook, wash and drain the beans, then place them in a large saucepan and cover completely with fresh cold water. Do not add salt at this stage as it will cause the beans to harden.

Bring the beans to the boil then lower the heat and simmer them for 20 to 30 minutes, or until tender. Drain and set aside.

Heat the oil in a large frying pan and add the mustard seeds. As they begin to pop, add the onion and curry leaves and sauté for 5 minutes until the onion is soft and just beginning to brown.

Add the green chile, turmeric powder and some salt. Mix thoroughly, then add the cooked beans. Stir well and cook over a low heat for 5 minutes. Add the coconut and stir well. Remove from the heat and serve.

200g/7oz black-eyed beans
2 tbsp oil
1 tsp mustard seeds
1 onion, finely sliced
10 curry leaves
1 green chile, slit
  lengthways
$^{1}/_{2}$ tsp turmeric powder
50g/2oz freshly grated or
  desiccated coconut
Salt

SERVES 4

CABBAGE AND POTATO THORAN

Cabbage thoran is perhaps the most common in Kerala. Cabbage is very cheap and needs few other ingredients to make it taste good, so people tend to buy it frequently. I have added soft browned cubes of potato to the dish because I like the way they contrast with the crisp, crunchy cabbage.

Heat 3 tablespoons of the oil in a large frying pan or wok. Add the potatoes and cook over a medium heat, stirring, for 10 to 15 minutes or until browned. Add salt to taste then set the potatoes aside on kitchen paper to drain.

In the same pan, heat the remaining 2 tablespoons of oil. Add the mustard seeds and, as they begin to pop, add the curry leaves and urad dal. Cook, stirring, until the urad dal turns golden.

Add the onions and green chile. Raise the heat to high and cook for 1 minute, then lower the heat right down and continue cooking for a further 5 minutes or until the onions are soft.

Add the turmeric and a little salt to taste. Stir in the shredded cabbage, cover and cook over a low heat, stirring occasionally, for 15 to 20 minutes or until the cabbage is soft.

Mix the browned potatoes into the cabbage. Remove from the heat, stir in the coconut, and serve.

5 tbsp oil
100g/3½oz potatoes, peeled and cubed
1 tsp mustard seeds
10 curry leaves
1 tsp urad dal
100g/3½oz onions, finely sliced
1 green chile, slit lengthways
1 tsp turmeric powder
200g/7oz cabbage, finely shredded
50g/2oz freshly grated or desiccated coconut
Salt

SERVES 4

DRUMSTICK THORAN

In Kerala, drumstick or muringakol is a very familiar vegetable and on sale in every market. Its flavour, texture and appearance are all attractions for its use in traditional dishes such as avial, sambar and lentil curry. My mother has her own ideas about everything, though, and she thinks drumsticks taste better cooked dry with freshly grated but juicy coconut. She taught me how to make this dish a long time ago and it remains a favourite of mine.

In a large saucepan of boiling water, cook the chopped drumsticks over a medium heat for 10 minutes, then drain and set aside to cool.

Halve each piece of drumstick and scoop out the flesh using a spoon or knife, discarding the skin. Place the fleshy parts in a bowl and set aside.

Heat the oil in a large frying pan. Add the green chiles, mustard seeds, curry leaves and a little salt and cook, stirring, until the mustard seeds begin to pop. Add the shallots and cook over a medium heat for 10 minutes, stirring occasionally.

Lower the heat and add the drumstick flesh. Cook, stirring, for a further 10 minutes. Mix in the coconut and serve hot.

450g/1lb drumsticks,
  chopped
3 tbsp oil
2 green chiles, slit
  lengthways
1 tsp mustard seeds
A few curry leaves
100g/3½ oz shallots,
  finely chopped
50g/2oz freshly grated
  or desiccated coconut
Salt

SERVES 4

TINDORI THORAN

This is the most popular thoran in our restaurants, even though most people are not familiar with tindori, a vegetable that looks rather like a miniature cucumber. The inclusion of cashew nuts makes this combination particularly crunchy, and therefore it is very different from the dishes people have come to expect from Indian restaurants.

Quarter the tindori lengthways. Bring a medium-sized saucepan of water to the boil and add $\frac{1}{2}$ teaspoon of turmeric, plus a little salt. Add the tindori and simmer for 5 minutes. Drain and set aside.

In a large frying pan, heat 2 tablespoons of the oil. Add the cashews and stir-fry them until golden. Remove the nuts from the pan and set aside to drain on kitchen paper.

Add another 3 tablespoons of the oil to the frying pan and place over a medium heat. Add the mustard seeds and, as they begin to pop, add the curry leaves, red chiles and chopped onion. Cook, stirring, for 5 minutes until the onion softens.

Stir in the remaining $\frac{1}{2}$ teaspoon of turmeric, season to taste with salt, then cook for another 2 minutes. Add the tindori and cashews and continue cooking for another 3 to 4 minutes, stirring constantly.

Remove the pan from the heat and add the coconut. Mix well, then transfer to a serving dish and serve hot.

500g/1lb 2oz tindori
1 tsp turmeric powder
5 tbsp oil
50g/2oz raw cashew nuts
1$\frac{1}{2}$ tbsp mustard seeds
10 curry leaves
2 dried red chiles
1 onion, finely chopped
200g/7oz freshly grated or
*   desiccated coconut*
Salt

SERVES 6

GREEN BEAN THORAN

Heat the oil in a large frying pan or wok. Add the mustard seeds and, as they begin to pop, add the curry leaves, urad dal and dried chiles. Cook, stirring, until the urad dal turns golden.

Add the onions and stir-fry for 5 minutes or until the onions are soft. Add the green chiles and turmeric powder and cook for another 2 minutes.

Stir in the beans and 4 tablespoons of water. Lower the heat right down, cover the pan and cook for 10 minutes, stirring occasionally.

Add the coconut and some salt to taste. Raise the heat to medium and stir-fry the mixture for 5 minutes. Remove from the heat and serve.

4 tbsp oil
1 tsp mustard seeds
10 curry leaves
1 tsp urad dal
2 dried red chiles
100g/3½ oz onions, finely chopped
3 green chiles, split lengthways
1 tsp turmeric powder
200g/7oz green beans, finely chopped
50g/2oz freshly grated or desiccated coconut
Salt

SERVES 4

SPINACH BHAJI

Called palak or sag in Hindi, spinach is a favourite with many North Indian people. They cook it in a variety of ways, including palak paneer (spinach with cheese) and sag aloo (spinach with potato), dishes that are well known even in Britain. In South India we have a red variety of spinach called cheera — it is not widely available in the West, where I think people are missing out on a really delicious vegetable. Here is my favourite way of eating spinach: cooked dry with the rich flavours of garlic and tomato, a method given to me by chef Narayan from our restaurants. You can eat this with bread, as a side dish or simply on its own.

Using a pestle and mortar, finely grind the green chile and ginger, adding a spoonful of water if needed to form a paste. Set aside.

Heat the oil in a large frying pan over a medium heat. Add the sliced garlic and cook for 30 seconds, then add the onion, stir and cook until the onion turns slightly golden at the edges.

Add the chile powder, turmeric and some salt, stir and cook for another minute. Add the tomatoes and cook for 5 minutes, stirring, until the tomatoes break down completely. Stir in the paste of green chile and ginger, then the bell pepper. Cover and cook for 5 minutes, stirring frequently.

Add the spinach and cook uncovered for 5 to 8 minutes, stirring, until the spinach is wilted. Remove from the heat and serve hot.

1 green chile
2.5cm/1in cube fresh ginger, peeled and chopped
2 tbsp oil
2 cloves garlic, sliced
1 onion, finely chopped
1/2 tsp chile powder
1/2 tsp turmeric powder
2 tomatoes, roughly chopped
1/2 red bell pepper, seeded and chopped
400g/14oz fresh spinach, tough stalks removed
Salt

SERVES 4

GREEN PEA MASALA

A simple dish that is made all over Kerala, green pea masala is one of the few vegetarian or vegan dishes that is easy to find in the restaurants. It is very peppery and makes a great meal served with flat bread.

Heat the oil in a large saucepan. Add the mustard seeds and, as they begin to pop, add the onions and a little salt to taste and cook until soft.

Add the ground coriander, turmeric and chile powder. Mix well, then add the tomatoes and 4 tablespoons of water and cook for 2 minutes.

Stir in the peas and pepper. Cover the pan and cook for 15 minutes or until the peas are tender.

Mix in the fresh coriander and add more pepper to taste. Cook for a further 2 minutes, then serve, garnished with fresh coriander if desired.

2 tbsp oil
1 tsp mustard seeds
100g/3½ oz onions
1 tsp ground coriander
1 tsp turmeric powder
½ tsp chile powder, or to taste
100g/3½ oz tomatoes, thickly sliced
300g/10oz peas, defrosted if frozen
1 tsp ground pepper, or to taste
2 tbsp chopped fresh coriander, plus a few sprigs extra to garnish (optional)
Salt

SERVES 4

BHINDI KICHADI

Cut the okra into 1cm/$\frac{1}{2}$ in pieces and set aside. Place
the ingredients for the spice paste into a grinder,
then process them for 1 minute or until roughly
ground. Set aside.

Heat the oil in large frying pan and fry the okra
until brown. Remove the okra from the pan and drain
on kitchen paper. Set aside.

Place the yogurt in a mixing bowl and beat with a
fork. Add the cooked okra, spice paste, a little
salt and mix well.

Reheat the oil remaining in the pan. Add the mustard
seeds and, as they begin to pop, add the curry
leaves. Cook for 1 minute then pour the mixture over
the okra. Stir well and serve at room temperature.

200g/7oz okra
5 tbsp oil
200g/7oz plain yogurt
$\frac{1}{2}$ tsp mustard seeds
10 curry leaves
Salt

For the spice paste:
100g/3$\frac{1}{2}$ oz freshly
  grated or desiccated
  coconut
1 green chile
1 clove garlic
1 tsp mustard powder

SERVES 4

BHINDI TOMATO SALAD

Cut the okra into 1cm/$\frac{1}{2}$ in pieces and set aside. Using
a pestle and mortar, finely grind the ingredients
for the spice paste and set aside.

Heat 4 tablespoons of the oil in a large frying pan
and cook the okra until brown. Remove from the heat,
drain on kitchen paper and set aside.

In the same pan, place the tomatoes and sugar and cook
for 5 minutes. Add the okra, the spice paste and a
little salt, then simmer for 2 to 3 minutes.

Meanwhile, heat 1 tablespoon of oil in a small pan.
Add the mustard seeds and, as they begin to pop, add
the curry leaves. Cook for 1 minute then pour the
contents of the pan over the okra mixture. Stir
well, transfer the mixture to a serving dish and
serve hot or cold.

5 tbsp oil
200g/7oz okra
300g/10$\frac{1}{2}$ oz tomatoes,
  finely chopped
A pinch of sugar
$\frac{1}{2}$ tsp mustard seeds
10 curry leaves
Salt

For the spice paste:
1 green chile
1 clove garlic
1 tsp mustard powder

SERVES 4

bhindi kichadi

GREEN MANGO AND SHALLOT SALAD

To my mind, the flesh of a mango is always much the same: it is the skin that distinguishes it. For this recipe, which uses unripened fruit, you can peel the mango if you like, but I prefer to eat it with the skin on.

Heat the oil in a frying pan or wok. Add the mustard seeds and, as they begin to pop, add the urad dal and curry leaves. Cook, stirring, until the urad dal turns golden.

Add the shallots and stir-fry for 5 minutes, until the shallots are shiny and translucent.

Stir in the chile powder, turmeric and some salt. Add the lemon juice and vinegar and mix well.

Remove the pan from the heat and transfer the mixture to a large bowl. Toss the cubes of cucumber and mango with the shallot mixture then serve, garnished with coconut slices.

2 tbsp oil
1 tsp mustard seeds
1 tsp urad dal
A few curry leaves
100g/3½ oz shallots, halved
A large pinch of chile powder
A large pinch of turmeric powder
3 tbsp lemon juice
3 tbsp white vinegar
200g/7oz cucumber, cubed
200g/7oz unripe mango, cubed
50g/2oz coconut slices
Salt

SERVES 4

GUAVA SALAD

Cut the guava into slices. Peel the mango and cut the flesh into strips. Peel and slice the avocado. Finely slice the shallots and chop the salad leaves.

Place all the fruit and vegetables in a large salad bowl. Add the lemon juice, chat masala, chile powder and salt to taste and toss gently before serving.

1 unripe guava
1 ripe mango
1 firm avocado
8 shallots
200g/7oz salad leaves
Juice of 1 lemon
1 tsp chat masala
A pinch of chile powder
Salt

SERVES 4

vegetable curries & soups

BRINJAL CURRY

Aubergine and tomato is a wonderful combination and this particular blend of spices brings out the subtle flavour of the aubergine. Brinjal is the Indian word for aubergine and this curry is a very popular dish in Keralan homes and restaurants. It can be served with salad and chapatis or ari pathiri.

Cut the aubergine into 2cm/$\frac{3}{4}$ in cubes and soak them in cold water for 10 minutes. Drain the aubergine and pat dry with kitchen paper.

In a large frying pan, heat 4 tablespoons of the oil over a medium heat. Add the aubergine and a little salt and cook for 10 minutes or until the aubergine is brown and soft. Drain the aubergine on kitchen paper and set aside in a warm place.

Heat the remaining tablespoon of oil in the same pan. Add the mustard seeds and, as they begin to pop, add the curry leaves and urad dal. Cook, stirring, for a few minutes or until the dal is golden, then add the onions and a little salt and cook until the onions are brown, stirring occasionally.

Add the tomatoes, tomato paste, chile powder, ground coriander and turmeric powder and mix well. Add the aubergine and cook for a further 5 minutes, stirring occasionally, until the tomatoes break down.

Transfer the mixture to a serving dish, garnish with the fresh coriander leaves, if using, and serve.

300g/10$\frac{1}{2}$ oz aubergine
5 tbsp oil
1 tsp mustard seeds
20 curry leaves
1 tsp urad dal
150g/5oz onions, finely sliced
200g/7oz tomatoes
1 tbsp tomato paste
$\frac{1}{2}$ tsp chile powder
$\frac{1}{2}$ tsp ground coriander
$\frac{1}{2}$ tsp turmeric powder
A few fresh coriander leaves, to garnish (optional)
Salt

SERVES 4

BAGAR BAINGAN

The inspiration for this dish was a well-known Hyderabadi preparation of quartered baby aubergines stuffed with spices which I found too dry and oily. I adjusted it to suit my style of cooking and added characteristic South Indian ingredients such as coconut and yogurt. In this way the aubergine maintains its integrity in the dish and the spicing is not too strong.

Cut the aubergines into 2.5cm/1in cubes and soak them in a bowl of cold, salted water for 10 minutes.

Meanwhile, place the coriander seeds and dried red chile in a frying pan and toast for 2 to 3 minutes over a medium heat. Transfer to a spice mill, grind to a fine powder and set aside.

Heat 1 tablespoon of the oil in the frying pan, add the onion and whole green chiles and cook until the onion is brown. Remove from the heat and set aside until the mixture is cool.

Meanwhile, drain and pat dry the aubergine. Place the cooled onion mixture, spice powder, yogurt and coconut in a blender and process for 3 to 4 minutes or until very smooth.

Rinse out the frying pan, then heat 2 tablespoons of oil in it. Add the mustard seeds and curry leaves and, as the mustard seeds begin to pop, add the aubergine and a little salt. Stir-fry for 5 to 10 minutes over a medium heat until the aubergine is light brown and soft.

Meanwhile, using a blender, grind the cashew nuts and cream to a smooth sauce and set aside.

Gently stir the onion sauce into the aubergine and cook over a low heat until the aubergine is very tender. Remove from the heat and transfer to a serving dish. Pour over the cashew cream and serve.

2 aubergines
1 tbsp coriander seeds
1 dried red chile
3 tbsp oil
1 onion, thickly sliced
2 green chiles
200ml/7floz plain yogurt
50g/2oz freshly grated
or desiccated coconut
1 tsp mustard seeds
A few curry leaves
25g/1oz raw cashew nuts
2 tbsp single cream
Salt

SERVES 4

RASA VANGI

A popular aubergine dish from Tamil Nadu, rasa vangi takes its sour flavour from a delicious combination of tamarind and onion. Fennel, which is not often found in Keralan cooking, makes a special contribution to the taste.

Cut the aubergines into 2.5cm/1in cubes and soak them in a bowl of cold, salted water for 10 minutes. Drain and pat dry with kitchen paper.

In a small saucepan, bring 225ml/8floz of water to the boil, add the tamarind pulp and simmer for 15 minutes. Sieve the mixture into a small bowl, using the back of a spoon to push the pulp through the mesh. Discard the stones and any hard skin. Set the tamarind liquid aside.

Heat the oil in a large saucepan. Add the mustard seeds and, as they begin to pop, add the onion, green chiles, ginger, fennel seeds, curry leaves and fenugreek seeds. Mix well and cook for 5 minutes over a medium heat until the onion begins to brown.

Add the ground coriander, turmeric and chile powders and stir thoroughly. Add the cubed aubergines, mix well and cook for 10 minutes, stirring frequently.

Add the tamarind liquid and a little salt, stirring well. Raise the heat, bring the mixture to a boil and simmer for 10 minutes until the sauce thickens.

Cover the pan, lower the heat and cook for a further 5 to 10 minutes or until the aubergines are well cooked. Serve hot.

2 aubergines
6 tbsp tamarind pulp
4 tbsp oil
1 tsp mustard seeds
1 onion, chopped
2 green chiles, finely chopped
2.5cm/1in cube fresh ginger, peeled and finely sliced
1 tsp fennel seeds
A few curry leaves
A large pinch of fenugreek seeds
2 tsp ground coriander
1 tsp turmeric powder
$\frac{1}{2}$ tsp chile powder
Salt

SERVES 4

BROCCOLI CURRY

Most people seem to enjoy broccoli. I thought it would be interesting to combine it with Indian spices, so I devised this dish, which is simple to make and good to eat. Customers in our restaurants like it a lot.

In a frying pan, heat 1 tablespoon of the oil or ghee and cook the sesame and poppy seeds for 2 minutes over a medium heat, stirring. Add the coconut and ginger and sauté until brown. Then add the peanuts, chile powder, turmeric and some salt. Mix well and continue cooking for another minute.

Remove from the heat and place the contents of the pan in a spice mill or grinder. Process the mixture for about 3 minutes to give a fine paste.

Heat the remaining 2 tablespoons of oil or ghee in a large saucepan. Add the sliced onion and cook for 2 to 3 minutes, then add the tomatoes and continue cooking for another 5 minutes or until most of the juices have evaporated.

Stir in the coconut paste, then the broccoli and green chiles and cook, stirring gently, for 5 minutes. Add 450ml/16floz of water, then cover and simmer for 10 minutes, stirring occasionally.

Taste and add more salt if required, then bring the mixture to a boil and cook until the broccoli is tender, stirring occasionally. Serve hot.

3 tbsp oil or ghee
2 tbsp sesame seeds
1 tbsp poppy seeds
50g/2oz freshly grated or
    desiccated coconut
2.5cm/1in cube fresh
    ginger, peeled and
    finely sliced
50g/2oz raw peanuts, skins
    removed
$\frac{1}{2}$ tsp chile powder
$\frac{1}{2}$ tsp turmeric powder
1 onion, finely sliced
2 tomatoes, chopped
500g/1lb 2oz broccoli,
    cut into chunks
3 green chiles
Salt

SERVES 4

GREEN BEAN CURRY

Another dish of my devising, and one of the simplest in the book, this recipe uses green beans, which in Kerala tend to be used only in dry dishes such as thoran and served as a salad. I however wanted to cook them in a sauce. If you want to use frozen beans and need to defrost them quickly, place them in a bowl of boiled water for 5 minutes.

Heat the oil in a large saucepan over a medium heat. Add the green chiles, ginger, curry leaves, mustard seeds, turmeric and chile powder and cook, stirring, for 1 minute. Add the onion and continue cooking for 4 to 5 minutes or until it is lightly browned.

Stir in the green beans, tomatoes and 4 tablespoons of water. Cover and cook for 10 to 15 minutes over a low heat, stirring occasionally, until the beans are soft and tender.

Add the coconut, then some salt and pepper to taste and mix well before serving.

4 tbsp oil
12 green chiles, halved
2.5cm/1in cube fresh
   ginger, peeled and
   finely chopped
10 curry leaves
2 tsp mustard seeds
1 tsp turmeric powder
$\frac{1}{2}$ tsp chile powder
1 onion, finely sliced
400g/14oz green beans,
   trimmed and cut in
   half, or 500g/1lb 2oz
   frozen beans, defrosted
2 tomatoes, finely chopped
50g/2oz freshly grated
   or desiccated coconut
Salt and ground pepper

SERVES 4

CABBAGE PARIPPU CURRY

Bring 300ml/10½ floz of water to the boil in a saucepan. Add the turmeric, then the lentils. Simmer for 15 minutes or until the lentils are well cooked and all the water has been absorbed.

Place the cabbage in a separate pan with 2 tablespoons of water and a little salt to taste. Cover and cook for 15 minutes or until the cabbage is tender but not soggy. Drain off any excess water.

Meanwhile, heat the oil in a large saucepan and, when hot, add the mustard seeds. As they begin to pop, add the urad dal and red chiles. When the dal turns golden, add the curry leaves and the cooked lentils and fry for 2 to 3 minutes.

Add the cooked cabbage and coconut and cook until all the water has evaporated. Serve immediately.

½ tsp turmeric powder
150g/5oz yellow split lentils
500g/1lb 2oz cabbage, chopped
1½ tsp oil
1 tsp mustard seeds
2 tsp urad dal
2 dried red chiles, finely chopped
A few curry leaves
2 tbsp freshly grated or desiccated coconut
Salt

SERVES 4

BEET PACHADI

In a spice mill, place the coconut, chiles, ginger and ground mustard and grind finely. Set aside.

If using raw beetroot, cut into wedges or cubes, cook in a saucepan of boiling water for 20 minutes or until tender, then drain and set aside; if using cooked beetroot, cut into wedges or cubes, rinse in a colander under cold water and set aside to drain.

In a large frying pan or wok, heat the oil. Add the mustard seeds and, as they begin to pop, add the curry leaves. Stir in the beetroot, chile powder, turmeric and a little salt and cook for 10 minutes over a medium heat, stirring frequently.

Mix in the coconut mixture. Lower the heat, cover and cook for 10 minutes, stirring often. Remove from the heat and stir in the yogurt. Serve hot or cold.

100g/3½ oz fresly grated or desiccated coconut
2 green chiles
2.5cm/1in cube fresh ginger, chopped
1 tsp ground mustard seeds
4 large raw or cooked beetroot, peeled
2 tbsp oil
2 tsp mustard seeds
10 curry leaves
1 tsp chile powder
1 tsp turmeric powder
225ml/8floz yogurt
Salt

SERVES 4

CORN BHAJI

If using fresh sweetcorn, wash and simmer it in a pan of water for 5 to 10 minutes until tender, then drain and set aside. If using frozen sweetcorn, simmer for 15 minutes, then drain and set aside.

Meanwhile, place the coconut and half the cashew nuts in a grinder with 200ml/7floz of water. Process for 5 minutes, then set aside.

Heat the oil in a large saucepan and add the mustard seeds. As they begin to pop, add the green chiles, ginger and curry leaves. Lightly sauté for about 2 minutes, stirring.

Add the onions and cook until golden brown. Add the tomato paste, chile powder, turmeric, a little salt and the ground coconut mixture. Mix well and cook for 5 minutes over a low heat.

Add the bell peppers and cook for 2 minutes, then add the cooked sweetcorn and the remaining cashew nuts and cook for a further 5 minutes. Remove from the heat and serve hot.

450g/1lb fresh or frozen sweetcorn kernels
100g/3$^1/_2$oz freshly grated or desiccated coconut
100g/3$^1/_2$oz raw cashew nuts
2 tbsp oil
$^1/_2$ tsp mustard seeds
3 green chiles, slit lengthways
2.5cm/1in cube ginger, peeled and finely chopped
10 curry leaves
2 onions, finely sliced
1 tbsp tomato paste
$^1/_2$ tsp chile powder
$^1/_2$ tsp turmeric powder
$^1/_2$ green bell pepper, seeded and finely chopped
$^1/_2$ red bell pepper, seeded and finely chopped
Salt

SERVES 4

PEPPER MASALA

I created this dish during a recent visit to my mother's house in India. It is based on something she made with hot green chiles, but I have modified the recipe to make it easier on the palate. The full sweetness of the peppers is brought out as they slowly caramelize with the onions and tomato paste. I find that the sweet richness of this dish creates an amazing balance to the hot spiciness of the other dishes served at a meal. It is best accompanied by plain basmati rice or chapati.

Using and peste and mortar, crush the garlic cloves and ginger together to give a fine paste.

Heat the oil in a large saucepan over a medium heat. Add the curry leaves, cumin and cloves and cook for 1 minute or until the cumin seeds turn golden. Add the onions and some salt to taste, stir and cook for 5 minutes or until the onions brown.

Add the paste of garlic and ginger to the saucepan and mix well. Then add the green chile, tomato paste, chile powder, ground coriander and turmeric. Stir well and cook for 3 to 4 minutes.

Add 6 to 7 tablespoons of water to the pan to loosen the mixture. Add the bell peppers, mix well and cook, uncovered, for 10 minutes or until the bell peppers begin to brown, stirring frequently.

Raise the heat under the saucepan to high and cook, stirring, for 2 minutes. Remove from the heat and leave to stand for 2 minutes before serving.

2 cloves garlic
1cm/$\frac{1}{2}$in cube fresh ginger, peeled
2 tbsp oil
About 20 curry leaves
$\frac{1}{2}$ tsp cumin seeds
5 cloves
200g/7oz onions, finely sliced
1 green chile
2 tbsp tomato paste
$\frac{1}{2}$ tsp chile powder, or to taste
$\frac{1}{2}$ tsp ground coriander
$\frac{1}{2}$ tsp turmeric powder
500g/1lb 2oz mixed bell peppers such as red, yellow and green, seeded and finely sliced
Salt

SERVES 4

potato curry

POTATO CURRY

Heat the oil in a large saucepan. Add the mustard
   seeds, dried chiles and curry leaves. As the mustard
   seeds begin to pop, add the onions and stir-fry
   until lightly browned.

Stir in the coriander, garam masala, turmeric and chile
   powder. Add the tomatoes and cook for 5 minutes.

Meanwhile, peel the potatoes and cut into wedges or
   cubes. Add them to the pan and cook over a gentle
   heat for 5 minutes, stirring constantly.

Pour in the coconut milk and 100ml/3½floz of water.
   Cook for 15 to 20 minutes until the potatoes are
   tender. Serve hot.

2 tbsp oil
1 tsp mustard seeds
2 dried red chiles
A few curry leaves
2 onions, chopped
½ tsp ground coriander
½ tsp garam masala
½ tsp turmeric powder
¼ tsp chile powder
2 tomatoes, quartered
400g/14oz potatoes
100ml/3½floz fresh or
   canned coconut milk

SERVES 4

POTATO MASALA

Place the potatoes in a large saucepan and cover with
   water. Add 1 teaspoon of the turmeric powder and
   some salt, bring to the boil and cook for 15 minutes
   or until the potatoes are soft. Drain and set aside.

In a large frying pan or wok, heat the oil over a
   medium heat. Add the mustard seeds and, as they
   begin to pop, add the urad dal and curry leaves.
   Stir-fry until the dal turns golden. Then add the
   onions, green chile and some salt and cook, stirring
   frequently, until the onions are golden brown.

Add the tomato paste, crushed ginger, chile powder and
   1 teaspoon of turmeric powder. Cook for 1 minute,
   then add the fresh tomatoes and cook for another
   2 minutes, stirring occasionally.

Lower the heat and mix in the bell pepper and peas.
   Cover and cook for 8 to 10 minutes. Then add the
   drained potatoes, stir thoroughly and serve.

600g/1lb 5oz potatoes,
   peeled and cubed
2 tsp turmeric powder
2 tbsp oil
2 tsp mustard seeds
1 tsp urad dal
10 curry leaves
200g/7oz onions, sliced
1 green chile, sliced
1 tbsp tomato paste
1cm/½in cube fresh
   ginger, crushed
½ tsp chile powder
100g/3½oz tomatoes, sliced
100g/3½oz bell pepper,
   seeded and sliced
100g/3½oz peas
Salt

SERVES 4

THAKALI CURRY

Finely slice half of the tomatoes and quarter the
remainder, keeping each batch separate.

Heat 2 tablespoons of the oil in a large saucepan. Add
the garlic, stir, and when brown, add the onions
and some salt. Cook, stirring, until the onions are
soft. Add the green chile and ginger, then lower
the heat and cook for 1 minute.

Stir in the chile powder, coriander, crushed cumin and
turmeric, then the sliced tomato and tomato paste.
Cook for 5 minutes, stirring constantly. Add the
tomato chunks and cook for a further 5 minutes.
Remove the pan from the heat and slowly mix in the
yogurt. Cover and set aside.

In a small frying pan, heat the remaining oil. Add
the mustard seeds and, as they begin to pop, add
the dried chiles and curry leaves and cook for
1 minute. Pour the mixture over the tomato curry
and mix well. Reheat before serving.

200g/7oz tomatoes
3 tbsp oil
2 cloves garlic, chopped
100g/3½oz onions, very
  finely sliced
1 green chile, slit
  lengthways
2.5cm/1in cube fresh
  ginger, peeled and very
  finely sliced
½ tsp chile powder
½ tsp ground coriander
½ tsp cumin seeds, crushed
½ tsp turmeric powder
1 tbsp tomato paste
500ml/18floz yogurt
1 tsp mustard seeds
2 dried red chiles
9-10 curry leaves
Salt

SERVES 4

RASA KOOTTU

A speciality of North Kerala, this dish is usually prepared after the monsoon season, when the garden produces its first harvest of vegetables. Rasa koottu is spicier than most Keralan dishes and has a more complex mix of flavours. Serve it with tamarind rice.

Prepare the vegetables: dice the onions; cut the carrots and potatoes into 5cm/2in chips; break the cauliflower into florets; and trim the beans into 5cm/2in pieces.

To make the spice paste, place all of the ingredients in a spice mill or blender and process for 1 minute or until smooth, adding a tablespoon of water if necessary. Set aside.

To make the curry, heat the oil in a large pan. Add the onions and green chile and cook over a medium heat for 5 minutes or until soft. Add the carrots, chile powder, ground coriander, turmeric and some salt and mix well. Cover and cook for 5 minutes, stirring occasionally.

Lower the heat and add the potatoes. Cover and cook, stirring occasionally, for another 10 to 15 minutes or until the carrots and potatoes are nearly cooked.

Add the cauliflower, green beans and spice paste. Mix well, then raise the heat to medium, cover the pan and cook for 10 to 15 minutes or until all of the vegetables are cooked.

Remove the pan from the heat and slowly add the coconut milk, stirring constantly. Return to the heat to warm through, stirring until the coconut milk is well blended, then serve.

100g/3½ oz onions
100g/3½ oz carrots,
 peeled
100g/3½ oz potatoes,
 peeled
100g/3½ oz cauliflower
100g/3½ oz fresh or
 frozen green beans
1 tbsp oil
1 green chile, finely
 sliced
½ tsp chile powder
½ tsp ground coriander
½ tsp turmeric powder
100ml/3½ floz fresh or
 canned coconut milk
Salt

For the spice paste:
100g/3½ oz tomatoes
2 cloves garlic
2.5cm/1in cube fresh
 ginger, peeled and
 chopped
1 green chile
½ tsp fennel seeds
2 cloves
2 cardamon pods

SERVES 4

SHALLOT CURRY

In a small saucepan, bring 340ml/12floz of water to the boil. Add the tamarind pulp and simmer for 5 minutes, then set aside to infuse for 30 minutes.

Wash the red dal and place it in a heavy saucepan with 450ml/16floz of water. Bring to the boil, then lower the heat, cover the pan and simmer for 30 minutes or until well cooked. Remove from the heat and set aside but do not drain.

Meanwhile, to make the spice paste, heat the oil in a large, heavy saucepan. Add the dried chiles, coriander seeds, chana dal, cumin and fenugreek seeds. Sauté for 2 to 3 minutes, then transfer the mixture to a blender. Add 6 of the shallots, plus the coconut and a little water and grind the mixture to a fine paste. Set aside.

Strain the tamarind liquid into a bowl and use the back of a wooden spoon to press as much pulp as possible through the sieve. Discard the stones and skin, then set the tamarind liquid aside.

To make the curry, heat the oil in a large, heavy saucepan. Add the mustard and cumin seeds, dried chile and curry leaves. As the mustard seeds begin to pop, add the remaining whole shallots and cook over a medium heat for 5 minutes.

Add the tamarind liquid, turmeric powder and a little salt to taste. Cover the pan and simmer for 7 to 10 minutes, or until the shallots are nearly cooked.

Add the undrained cooked dal and the spice paste to the pan. Mix well and cook for 5 minutes, or until the sauce thickens and the shallots are well cooked. Garnish with coriander leaves and serve hot.

50g/2oz tamarind pulp
75g/3oz red dal
2 tbsp oil
1 tbsp mustard seeds
1 tbsp cumin seeds
1 dried red chile
A few curry leaves
$\frac{1}{2}$ tsp turmeric powder
A small bunch of coriander
   leaves
Salt

For the spice paste:
2 tbsp oil
6 dried red chiles
3 tbsp coriander seeds
2 tbsp chana dal
1 tsp cumin seeds
A large pinch of fenugreek
   seeds
250g/9oz shallots, peeled
50g/2oz freshly grated or
   desiccated coconut

SERVES 4

VEGETABLE STEW

Served with appams, this vegetarian version of classic chicken or lamb stew makes a good breakfast dish. Adding a variety of vegetables is typical of the new style of home cooking found in India.

In a large saucepan, heat the ghee or butter, add the shallots and fry for 5 minutes until brown. Remove the pan from the heat and sprinkle the flour over the shallots. Mix well and return to a low heat.

Slowly add 450ml/16floz water, mixing well to avoid lumps. Stir in the tomato paste, chile powder, ground coriander and turmeric. Then add the potato, beans, carrots and peas and cook, covered, for 20 minutes or until all the vegetables are tender, stirring occasionally.

Remove the pan from the heat, pour in the coconut milk and stir for 2 minutes. Serve immediately.

1 tsp ghee or butter
12 shallots, cut into
*   wedges*
1½ tsp plain flour
3 tbsp tomato paste
½ tsp chile powder
½ tsp ground coriander
¼ tsp turmeric powder
250g/9oz potato, cut into
*   batons*
250g/9oz fresh green beans,
*   trimmed*
150g/5oz carrots,
*   cut into batons*
100g/3½oz fresh or frozen
*   peas, defrosted if*
*   frozen*
250ml/9floz fresh or canned
*   coconut milk*
Salt

SERVES 4

MORU KACHIATHU WITH GREEN BANANA AND MANGO

A vibrant yellow curry of ginger, onions and yogurt cooked with spices, moru kachiathu is a must for all Keralan meals. It is very simple to make but has an amazing flavour that enhances other foods. This recipe includes green banana and mango, additions popular at our restaurants, but in India moru kachiathu is generally eaten plain, more as a sauce than a curry. To turn it into a meal, serve it with lemon rice or appams.

Peel the green banana using a knife, then slice the flesh thinly. Bring a small saucepan of salted water to the boil. Add 1 teaspoon of the turmeric powder, then the banana and cook over a medium heat for 10 minutes. Drain and set aside.

In a large saucepan, heat the oil. Add the mustard seeds and, as they begin to pop, add the onion, curry leaves, red chiles and salt. Cook, stirring frequently, over a medium heat for 5 minutes or until the onion has browned.

Meanwhile, using a pestle and mortar, crush the ginger to a smooth paste. Add it to the onion mixture with the green chile, stir well and cook for 1 minute.

Add the remaining teaspoon of turmeric, mix thoroughly, then remove the pan from the heat. Gradually add the yogurt, banana and mango, stirring slowly and continuously. Return the pan to the heat for 1 minute, stirring constantly. Serve lukewarm.

1 small green banana or
*   plantain*
2 tsp turmeric powder
1 tbsp oil
1 tsp mustard seeds
1 small onion, finely
*   sliced*
20 curry leaves
2 dried red chiles
1 tsp salt
1cm/$\frac{1}{2}$in cube fresh
*   ginger, peeled and*
*   chopped*
1 green chile, slit
*   lengthways*
400ml/14floz yogurt
1 small ripe mango, peeled
*   and thinly sliced, or*
*   4 slices canned mango,*
*   thinly sliced*

SERVES 4

RIPE BANANA PACHADI

Using a spice mill or a pestle and mortar, grind
together the coconut, green chiles and mustard seeds
with 1 tablespoon of water to make a paste.

Peel the plantain and cut it into 2.5cm/1in pieces. In
a large saucepan, heat 3 tablespoons of the oil and
stir-fry the plantain for 5 minutes.

Add a little salt to taste and 125ml/4floz of water.
Reduce the heat, mix in the spice paste and cook
for 2 minutes. Add the yogurt and cook, stirring
constantly, for 5 minutes.

In a small frying pan, heat the remaining 1 tablespoon
of oil. Add the dried red chiles and curry leaves,
then pour the contents of the pan over the curry and
gently stir through. Serve hot.

50g/2oz freshly grated or
*   desiccated coconut*
2 green chiles
1 tsp mustard seeds
450g/1lb ripe plantain
4 tbsp oil
200ml/7floz plain yogurt
3 dried red chiles
A few curry leaves
Salt

SERVES 4

KADACHAKKA STEW

Heat the oil in a large saucepan. Add the mustard
seeds and, as they begin to pop, add the green
chiles, ginger and curry leaves and sauté for
2 minutes. Stir in the onions and cook for 5 minutes
over a medium heat or until the onions are soft.

Add the breadfruit, tomatoes and 450ml/16floz of water.
Mix well and cook for 15 to 20 minutes or until the
breadfruit is tender.

Lower the heat and add the coconut milk, stirring to
combine thoroughly. Serve hot.

4 tbsp oil
1 tsp mustard seeds
2 green chiles, slit
*   lengthways*
2.5cm/1in cube fresh
*   ginger, peeled and cut*
*   into fine strips*
A few curry leaves
3 onions, cut into chunks
450g/1lb breadfruit,
*   peeled and cut into*
*   chunks*
3 tomatoes, sliced
700ml/1 pint 4floz fresh or
*   canned coconut milk*

SERVES 4

PAPAYA PARIPPU CURRY

In a large saucepan of boiling salted water, cook the papaya, covered, over a medium heat for 15 minutes until the fruit is tender. Drain and set aside.

Meanwhile, wash the chana dal in cold water. In a small saucepan, bring 225ml/8floz of salted water to the boil, add the chana dal and cook, covered, for 10 to 15 minutes until well cooked. Set aside.

Using a spice mill or pestle and mortar, grind the coconut, green chile and fennel to a fine paste.

In a large frying pan, heat the oil. Add the mustard seeds and, as they begin to pop, add the onion and curry leaves. Stir well and cook over a medium heat until the onion is golden brown.

Add the ground coconut mixture, then reduce the heat and cook, stirring, for 2 to 3 minutes. Mix in the cooked papaya and chana dal and serve hot.

200g/7oz unripe papaya, peeled and cut into chunks
25g/1oz chana dal
50g/2oz freshly grated or desiccated coconut
1 green chile
1 tsp fennel seeds
2 tbsp oil
1 tsp mustard seeds
1 large onion, finely chopped
A few curry leaves
1 tsp turmeric powder
Salt

SERVES 4

CHANA MASALA

If using dried chickpeas, wash them and leave to soak
for 6 hours or overnight. To cook, drain and place
the chickpeas in a large saucepan of fresh water.
Bring to the boil and simmer for 3 hours or until
tender; alternatively, cook the chickpeas in a
pressure cooker for 45 minutes. Drain and set aside.
If using canned chickpeas, wash and drain them.

Heat the oil in a large saucepan, then add the onion
and cook for 5 to 7 minutes until browned. Stir
in the chopped tomatoes, then the ginger, ground
coriander, turmeric and chile powder and cook for
5 minutes over a low heat.

Add the cooked or canned chickpeas, cover and cook for
15 minutes, stirring occasionally. Garnish with the
chopped coriander leaves and serve hot.

*400g/14oz dried chickpeas,
  or 600g/1lb 5oz canned
  chickpeas*
3 tbsp oil
1 onion, sliced
2 tomatoes, finely chopped
*2.5cm/1in cube fresh
  ginger, peeled and cut
  into strips*
2 tsp ground coriander
1 tsp turmeric powder
$\frac{1}{2}$ tsp chile powder
*2 tbsp chopped coriander
  leaves*

SERVES 4

OLAN

Here is a very simple curry with limited spicing. An excellent choice for
people who do not like hot spices, it provides a good contrast of colour when
served as part of a meal and balances more fiery dishes.

If using dried beans, place them in a small pan, cover
with water and simmer for 30 minutes or until the
beans are well cooked. Drain and set aside. If using
canned beans, wash them well, drain and set aside.

In a large saucepan, bring 450ml/16floz of water to the
boil. Add the potato and a little salt and cook over
a medium heat for 10 minutes. Add the pumpkin and
green chiles, cover and cook for 10 minutes until
all the vegetables are tender.

Lower the heat under the pan and add the coconut milk,
stirring gently. Add the beans and curry leaves, mix
well and allow to beans to heat through. Serve warm.

*100g/3$\frac{1}{2}$oz black-eyed
  beans, dried or canned*
1 potato, peeled and cubed
*400g/14oz white or
  yellow pumpkin, peeled,
  seeded and cubed*
*2 green chiles, slit
  lengthways*
*200ml/7floz fresh or
  canned coconut milk*
A few curry leaves
Salt

SERVES 4

NADAN PARIPPU

Wash the moong dal thoroughly and set aside to drain. To make the spice paste, place the coconut and cumin seeds in a grinder with 225ml/8floz of water and process for 1 minute. Set the paste aside.

Half-fill a large saucepan with water and bring to the boil. Add the green chile and some salt, then the dal. Cook for 15 minutes or until the dal is very tender. Drain off any excess water, leaving the dal in the pan — you want to dal to be dry, thick and sticky, almost like mashed potato.

Add the coconut mixture to the cooked dal and stir well. Place over a low heat, bring to the boil and simmer for 5 minutes. Add the curry leaves and stir until well blended.

Remove the saucepan from the heat and serve the dal straight away; do not try to reheat or serve the dal at a later stage, as the curry will become far too starchy and thick if left standing.

200g/7oz moong dal
1 green chile, finely
*   chopped*
A few curry leaves
Salt

For the spice paste:
50g/2oz fresh coconut,
*   roughly chopped*
¼ tsp cumin seeds

SERVES 4

RASAM

Wash the red gram dal thoroughly and place in a heavy saucepan. Cover with water and add a pinch of salt. Bring the dal to the boil, cover and simmer over a low heat for 1 to 1$\frac{1}{2}$ hours until the dal is cooked. Set aside without draining.

Roughly break up the tamarind pulp with your hands and place the pieces in 450ml/16floz of warm water to soak for 10 minutes. Drain through a fine sieve into a small bowl, pushing the pulp through the sieve with the back of a spoon. Discard the stones and fibres and set the tamarind liquid aside.

Place the tomatoes, garlic and ginger in a blender and process for 1 minute.

In a large saucepan, heat the tamarind liquid over a medium heat for 5 minutes. Add the fresh coriander, green chile, turmeric, black pepper and the blended tomato mixture. Bring the soup to a boil and cook for 15 minutes, stirring occasionally, being careful not to let the mixture boil over. Add the cooked dal, stir well and add salt to taste. Remove from the heat and set aside.

In a frying pan, heat the oil, then add the mustard seeds and, as they begin to pop, add the dried chiles, cumin seeds, ground cumin, ground coriander, curry leaves and asafoetida. Fry for 1 minute, then pour the oil and spices over the soup. Stir through, garnish with the extra coriander leaves and serve.

50g/2oz red gram dal
100g/4oz tamarind pulp
2 tomatoes, chopped
4 cloves garlic
2.5cm/1in cube fresh ginger, peeled and finely sliced
A small bunch of fresh coriander, finely chopped, plus extra for garnishing
1 green chile, slit lengthways
1 tsp turmeric powder
$\frac{1}{2}$ tsp ground black pepper
3 tbsp oil
1 tsp mustard seeds
3 dried red chiles
1 tsp cumin seeds
$\frac{1}{2}$ tsp ground cumin
$\frac{1}{2}$ tsp ground coriander
A few curry leaves
A small pinch of asafoetida
Salt

SERVES 4

CHEERA SOUP

In a large saucepan, place the spinach and green chile. Cover and cook over a medium heat for 5 minutes or until the spinach is wilted but only half cooked. Remove from the heat and drain.

In another pan, bring some salted water to the boil, add the potato and simmer for 10 minutes or until tender. Drain and mash roughly.

Heat the oil in a frying pan and add half the sliced onion. Cook for 7 to 10 minutes, or until crisp and brown, stirring occasionally. Remove from the pan and set aside.

Heat the ghee or butter in a large saucepan. Add the rest of the onion, the cinnamon and cloves and sauté for 5 minutes or until the onions are soft.

Add the flour and mashed potato, mix well, and cook for 2 to 3 minutes.

Add the tomatoes and wilted spinach to the saucepan, then pour in 900ml/1 pint 12floz of water. Bring to the boil and simmer for 5 minutes over a medium heat, stirring constantly.

Pour into serving bowls, garnish with the chopped red bell pepper and crisp onions and serve hot.

400g/14oz fresh spinach, finely chopped
1 green chile, slit lengthways
1 potato, peeled and chopped
1 tbsp oil
1 large onion, finely sliced
1 tbsp ghee or butter
1 cinnamon stick
3 cloves
1 tbsp plain flour
2 tomatoes, quartered
½ red bell pepper, seeded and finely chopped
Salt

SERVES 4

DRUMSTICK SOUP

Drumsticks are one of the few South Indian vegetables not often seen in other parts of the world. This hearty soup makes the most of their unique meaty flavour and texture, which are enhanced by the use of fresh ginger.

In a large saucepan, heat the oil. Add the mustard seeds and, as they begin to pop, add the onion, green chiles, ginger and curry leaves. Sauté for 5 minutes over a low heat.

When the onions are soft, add the tomato, gram flour and a little salt. Cook, stirring, for 5 minutes.

Cut the drumsticks into 5cm/2in pieces. Add them to the pan with 500ml/18floz of water and bring the mixture to a boil. Lower the heat and simmer for 10 minutes. Stir well and serve hot.

2 tbsp oil
1 tsp mustard seeds
1 onion, finely sliced
2 green chiles
2.5cm/1in cube fresh
ginger, peeled and
sliced
A few curry leaves
1 tomato, finely chopped
2 tbsp gram (chickpea)
flour
3 drumsticks
Salt

SERVES 4

VEGETABLE SOUP

I like soups but did not really discover them until I left Kerala. In India, they tend to be the preserve of Christian and Jewish communities. This recipe comes from a family friend, a Christian lady in the village in which I grew up. Cinnamon, often used in Kerala, adds a delicious flavour.

In a frying pan, heat the ghee or butter, then add the onion and cook for 5 minutes or until brown. Remove from the heat and set aside.

In a large saucepan, place 700ml/1 pint 4floz of water, add a little salt and bring to the boil. Add the vegetables, onions, ground pepper, chile powder, turmeric and cinnamon. Cook over a medium heat for 30 minutes or until the vegetables are very soft and beginning to break down. Remove from the heat and allow to cool slightly.

Transfer the soup to a blender and process for 2 to 3 minutes to give a smooth liquid. Return to the saucepan and heat through briefly. Serve hot, with a small spoonful of ghee or butter in each bowl.

4 tbsp ghee or butter, plus extra for serving
100g/3½ oz onions, cut into small pieces
100g/3½ oz fresh green beans, cut into small pieces
100g/3½ oz cabbage, cut into small pieces
100g/3½ oz carrots, cut into small pieces
100g/3½ oz leeks, cut into small pieces
100g/3½ oz tomatoes, cut into small pieces
1 tsp ground pepper
¼ tsp chile powder
¼ tsp turmeric powder
A pinch of ground cinnamon
Salt

SERVES 4

eggs, poultry, meat & fish

MOTTA ROAST

In a saucepan of water, slowly bring the eggs to a boil and boil for 10 minutes until hard. Drain and cool. Remove the shells and set aside.

Heat the oil in a large pan and sauté the green chiles, ginger and curry leaves for 2 to 3 minutes. Add the onions and fry until half cooked.

Add the tomatoes, turmeric, chile powder and a little salt. Cook for 5 minutes or until thick. Add the whole eggs to the sauce and mix gently until they are covered with the mixture. Remove from the heat and serve hot with rice or appams.

6 large eggs
3 tbsp oil
4 green chiles, slit lengthways
2.5cm/1in cube fresh ginger, peeled and finely chopped
20 curry leaves
3 medium onions, finely sliced
3 tomatoes, sliced
$\frac{1}{4}$ tsp turmeric powder
$\frac{1}{4}$ tsp chile powder
Salt

SERVES 4

MOTTA THORAN

Break the eggs into a bowl and add a little salt. Whisk with a fork or hand whisk for about 2 minutes or until the eggs are well mixed and bubbles begin to form on the surface.

Heat the oil in a large frying pan, add the green chiles, ginger and curry leaves and stir-fry for 2 minutes until fragrant. Add the onions and cook for 5 minutes over a medium heat until the onions are half cooked.

Stir in the turmeric and chile powders. Add the beaten eggs and, using a wooden spoon, stir constantly for 5 minutes until scrambled. Remove from the heat and serve hot with plain rice.

3 large eggs
2 tbsp oil
2 green chiles, finely sliced
1cm/$\frac{1}{2}$in cube fresh ginger, peeled and finely sliced
10 curry leaves, roughly chopped
1 onion, finely chopped
$\frac{1}{4}$ tsp turmeric powder
$\frac{1}{4}$ tsp chile powder
Salt

SERVES 4

EGG CURRY

Egg dishes are very popular for breakfast and lunch in India. They are quick to cook and cheap, especially as many people keep their own hens. This recipe hails from Cochin and was given to me by one of the chefs in our restaurants.

To make the spice paste, place one-third of the finely chopped onion in a large frying pan or wok with the coconut, fresh chiles, tamarind, coriander seeds, asafoetida and cumin seeds. Toast for 5 minutes over a medium heat, stirring constantly. Remove from the heat and set aside to cool.

Transfer the toasted spice mixture to a grinder and grind for 2 to 3 minutes. Then, in a large, heavy saucepan, combine the ground spices with the rest of the finely chopped onion and 400ml/14floz of water. Bring the mixture to the boil, lower the heat and simmer for 5 minutes, stirring occasionally.

Add a little salt, then carefully break the eggs into the saucepan. Cover and cook for 5 minutes or until the eggs are done to your taste.

In a frying pan, heat the oil, then add the chopped onion and cook over a high heat, stirring, until brown. Remove from the heat and pour the contents of the frying pan over the eggs. Serve hot.

6 eggs
2 tbsp oil
1 onion, chopped

For the spice paste:
1 large onion, finely chopped
100g/3½ oz freshly grated or desiccated coconut
5-6 fresh red chiles
4 tbsp tamarind pulp
2 tsp coriander seeds
A pinch of asafoetida
A pinch of cumin seeds
Salt

SERVES 4

KOZHY MAPPAS

Not all Keralan food has coconut in it! But this chicken dish is certainly unusual in that it does not. It is a speciality from Kottayam, where the Christian community predominates, and is typical of the experimental style of cooking enjoyed by many of the home cooks there.

Heat the oil in a large frying pan or wok. When hot, add the green chiles, garlic, ginger, curry leaves, cinnamon, cardamon, peppercorns and cloves. Stir-fry the mixture over a medium heat until the garlic and ginger are brown.

Add the onion and stir-fry until the onion is a deep golden brown. Add the tomato, ground coriander, turmeric and chile powders and a little salt. Cook for 5 minutes until the tomato breaks down to give a thick sauce and is well combined with the spices.

Meanwhile, cut the chicken into 2.5cm/1in pieces. Add the chicken to the pan and stir well, until the chicken is covered with sauce. Pour in 225ml/8floz of water and mix thoroughly. Cover and cook for a further 10 minutes, stirring occasionally to prevent sticking and burning.

Reduce the heat under the pan to low, add the yogurt and mix well. Serve hot.

3 tbsp oil
2 green chiles, chopped
3 cloves garlic, finely sliced
2.5cm/1in cube fresh ginger, peeled and sliced
10 curry leaves
1 stick cinnamon
5 cardamon pods
5 black peppercorns
5 cloves
1 large onion, finely sliced
1 tomato, thickly sliced
1 tbsp ground coriander
1/4 tsp turmeric powder
1/4 tsp chile powder
400g/14oz chicken fillets
2 tbsp plain yogurt
Salt

SERVES 4

PEPPER CHICKEN

A speciality of Chettinad in Tamil Nadu, this dish is typical of the cooking of the Chettiar community. It has a very peppery flavour, which is unusual for a chicken dish, but I think that is precisely why many people like it. The mixture is quite dry and goes well with poories or ari pathiri.

Using a pestle and mortar, pound the garlic and ginger to a fine paste. Set aside.

Heat the oil in a large frying pan. Add the onions, curry leaves and green chile and cook over a medium heat until the onions are brown.

Add the garlic-ginger paste and cook for 5 minutes, stirring occasionally. Add the coriander, turmeric powder and some salt. Mix well and cook for a further 5 minutes.

Add the chicken to the frying pan, stir through, then add 225ml/8floz of water and the garam masala. Mix well, cover and cook over a low heat for 5 minutes, or until the chicken is cooked through.

Stir the ground pepper into the mixture, then remove the pan from the heat and serve.

3 cloves garlic, roughly chopped
2.5cm/1in cube fresh ginger, peeled and sliced
4 tbsp oil
2 medium onions, finely sliced
10 curry leaves
1 green chile, slit lengthways
1 tsp ground coriander
$\frac{1}{2}$ tsp turmeric powder
500g/1lb 2oz chicken, cubed
1 tsp garam masala
$\frac{1}{2}$ tsp ground pepper
Salt

SERVES 4

CHICKEN GREEN MASALA

Not a traditional dish, but a simple combination that is very popular with Indian chefs, who often make it for their own working lunches. It exemplifies the modern mix of South Indian home-style cooking with the ingredients of Bombay, a 'cuisine' that emerges when Keralan chefs go to work in the city and share flats with people from other parts of the country.

Place all the ingredients for the spice paste into a blender or grinder and process to a very fine paste. Set aside.

In a large saucepan, heat the oil then add the onions and cook over a medium heat for 5 minutes or until the onions are brown. Stir in the spice paste, reduce the heat and cook for a further 5 minutes.

Add the chicken, tomatoes and a little salt and mix well. Cover and cook gently for 10 minutes, stirring occasionally — do not allow the chicken to boil hard or it will become tough and stringy.

Remove the lid from the pan and continue cooking uncovered for a further 5 minutes or until the chicken is done. Serve hot.

2 tbsp oil
2 onions, finely chopped
1 medium chicken, cleaned and cut into small pieces
4 tomatoes, finely chopped
Salt

For the spice paste:
A large bunch of coriander leaves, roughly chopped
1 large onion, roughly chopped
10 green chiles, or to taste
5 cloves garlic
4cm/1½ in cube fresh ginger, peeled and chopped
2 cinnamon sticks, about 5cm/2in each
2 tsp coriander seeds
1 tsp cumin seeds
1 tsp peppercorns
1 tsp poppy seeds
¼ tsp turmeric powder
2 cardamon pods
2 cloves

SERVES 4

ATTU VARUVAL

Dry meat, chicken and fish dishes are a speciality of the toddy bars, or kallu shaps as they are known colloquially, where they are eaten with the fingers. So popular are these dishes in Kerala that people will go to the bars to enjoy them even if they are not interested in drinking. This one made from lamb is particularly spicy, contrasting nicely with the coconut.

Place 450ml/16floz of water in a large saucepan, add 1/2 teaspoon of the turmeric powder and 1 teaspoon of salt and bring to the boil. Add the lamb pieces and simmer uncovered for 15 minutes until the lamb is well cooked and the water has almost evaporated. Remove the pan from the heat and set aside.

Heat the oil in a large frying pan. Add the onions and cook until well browned. Add the mashed garlic, green chile, ground coriander and 1 1/2 teaspoons of turmeric. Mix well, then add the curry leaves and ginger. Cook, stirring, for 2 minutes.

Drain any excess water from the lamb and stir the meat into the onion mixture. Add the ground pepper and garam masala and stir-fry for 5 minutes, or until the mixture becomes quite dry.

Add the coconut and some salt to taste. Give a final stir, then remove from the heat and serve.

2 tsp turmeric powder
500g/1lb 2oz lamb, cut into small pieces
6 tbsp oil
2 medium onions, finely sliced
3 cloves garlic, mashed
1 green chile
1/2 tsp ground coriander
10 curry leaves
2.5cm/1in cube fresh ginger, peeled and finely chopped
1/2 tsp ground pepper
1/2 tsp garam masala
100g/3 1/2 oz freshly grated or desiccated coconut
Salt

SERVES 4

LAMB STEW

You will find this mild curry, a Christian dish particularly associated with Easter, in most restaurants in Kerala. It is a good match for highly spiced dishes and is traditionally eaten with appams.

Place all the ingredients for the spice paste in a grinder and process for 2 to 3 minutes to give a fine paste. Set aside.

To cook the lamb, heat 1 tablespoon of the ghee or oil in a large pan. Add the meat and stir-fry for 2 to 3 minutes until the lamb is sealed. Stir in the spice paste, then add the coconut milk, two-thirds of the onions, the tomatoes, green chiles and some salt. Mix well and simmer for 20 minutes, stirring frequently, until the lamb is cooked through.

Add the lime juice and coriander leaves to the lamb and mix well. Return the mixture to the boil, simmer for 2 minutes, then remove the pan from the heat.

In a frying pan, heat the remaining 2 tablespoons of ghee or oil and fry the rest of the onion until golden brown. Pour the contents of the frying pan into the lamb stew and stir through. Serve hot.

3 tbsp ghee or oil
500g/1lb 2oz lamb, cubed
200ml/7floz fresh or
  canned coconut milk
3 onions, finely chopped
3 tomatoes, chopped
6 green chiles, or to
  taste, slit lengthways
Juice of 1 lime
1 tbsp chopped coriander
  leaves
Salt

For the spice paste:
10 cloves garlic
20 peppercorns
2 cinnamon sticks, about
  5cm/2in each
1 tbsp freshly grated or
  desiccated coconut
1 tbsp coriander seeds
1/4 tsp poppy seeds
A pinch of ground cumin

SERVES 4

BEEF CHILE

Beef is still not frequently eaten in India. Kerala, with its Christian community, is somewhat of an exception, but you are more likely to see dishes such as this one in restaurants rather than private homes. Christian families like to serve beef chile at weddings.

Grind the ginger and garlic to a fine paste using a pestle and mortar. Set aside.

Place 450ml/16floz of water and the turmeric in a large saucepan and bring to the boil. Add the meat and 1 teaspoon of salt. Lower the heat to medium and simmer for 10 minutes.

In a large frying pan, heat the oil, then add the onions and cook until golden brown. Add the ginger and garlic paste, mix well and continue cooking for 2 minutes over a medium heat.

Add the tomatoes, coriander, garam masala and a little salt, stirring well. Cook for 10 minutes, stirring frequently, to give a thick sauce.

Add the green chiles and another 450ml/16floz of water to the onion mixture and stir well. Add the beef and red bell pepper, bring to the boil, then lower the heat and simmer for 5 minutes. Stir in the fresh coriander and serve immediately.

2.5cm/1in cube fresh
  ginger, peeled and
  sliced
2 cloves garlic
½ tsp turmeric powder
500g/1lb 2oz beef
steak, cut into chunks
4 tbsp oil
2 large onions, chopped
2 tomatoes, finely chopped
1 tsp ground coriander
1 tsp garam masala
4 green chiles, slit
  lengthways
1 red bell pepper, seeded
  and finely sliced
A handful of chopped fresh
  coriander
Salt

SERVES 4

MEEN MOLLY

The inclusion of lemon juice, vinegar and garlic in this famous curry reflects the Christian contribution to Keralan cuisine — the Hindus would tend to use tamarind for sourness in this type of dish. Normally Keralan fish curries are very hot, but this is an exception, mild and light to eat. In India, this would be cooked using freshly made coconut milk, therefore it is considered an elaborate recipe for special occasions.

Clean the fish in a bowl of salted water and cut the flesh into 2.5cm/1in cubes.

Heat the oil in a large frying pan. Add the tomatoes, onion, curry leaves, green chiles and ginger. Cook over a moderate heat for 5 minutes or until the onions are lightly browned. Add the turmeric and chile powder and mix well.

Add 200ml/7floz of water, raise the heat to high and boil for 2 minutes. Then lower the heat right down and carefully stir the coconut milk into the curry. Simmer gently for a further 5 minutes.

Add the cubed fish and cook over a medium heat for 10 minutes, stirring occasionally. Mix in the lemon juice and vinegar, then remove from the heat. Serve with plain boiled rice.

400g/14oz king fish
4 tbsp oil
2 tomatoes, quartered
1 onion, sliced
20 curry leaves
2 green chiles, slit lengthways
2.5cm/1in cube fresh ginger, peeled and sliced
$1/2$ tsp turmeric powder
$1/4$ tsp chile powder
200ml/7floz fresh or canned coconut milk
1 tbsp lemon juice
1 tbsp vinegar
Salt

SERVES 4

MEEN PAPPAS

Unlike the previous recipe for meen molly, this is considered an everyday dish in India, one that you would find cooked in homes rather than in restaurants. It is derived from the Hindu style of vegetarian cooking, in which ground coconut preparations are typical.

Clean the fish in a bowl of salted water. Cut the flesh into 1cm/½ in slices and set aside.

Place the grated or desiccated coconut in a grinder. Add 100ml/3½ floz of water and process to a paste.

Heat the oil in a large pan, then add the onion, green chiles, ginger and curry leaves and stir-fry until the onions turn brown. Add the chile and turmeric powders and cook for another 2 minutes.

Add the tomatoes and cook for 5 minutes or until the tomatoes are very soft and break down into the spices. Stir in 225ml/8floz of water, then bring to the boil and simmer for 5 minutes.

Lower the heat under the pan and add the fish pieces, then the coconut paste. Stir carefully and simmer for 5 to 7 minutes or until the sauce thickens and the fish is cooked. Add the vinegar and remove from the heat. Serve hot.

400g/14oz king fish
100g/3½ oz freshly grated
   or desiccated coconut
4 tbsp oil
1 onion, finely diced
3 green chiles, finely
   sliced
2.5cm/1in cube fresh
   ginger, peeled and
   finely diced
A few curry leaves
1 tsp chile powder
1 tsp turmeric powder
2 tomatoes, sliced
3 tbsp vinegar
Salt

SERVES 4

MEEN PORICHATHU

This is a very common way of eating fish in Kerala both in the home and at restaurants. It is a dry mixture served rather like a dry vegetable side dish to complement saucier meat and chicken dishes.

Place all the ingredients for the spice paste in a grinder or blender. Process for 2 to 3 minutes or until a very fine sauce is achieved. Set aside.

Wash the fish under cold water then pat dry with kitchen paper. With a very sharp knife, make some slashes about 2.5cm/1in apart along the whole length of the fish — not too deeply, just enough to break the skin and cut slightly into the flesh.

Place the fish on a baking tray. Spread all the spice paste all over the fish, ensuring that it penetrates well into the cuts. Set the fish aside to marinate for 15 to 20 minutes.

When ready to cook, heat 2 tablespoons of the oil in a large frying pan. Add the finely sliced onion and cook for 5 to 6 minutes over a very high heat until the onion is well browned and crisp. Remove the onion from the pan and drain on kitchen paper.

Using the same pan, add the remaining 4 tablespoons of oil and place over a low heat. Carefully place the whole fish into the pan, cover and cook for about 6 minutes on each side — only turn the fish once or twice during cooking, as turning it more often will encourage it to fall apart. Cook until the skin is brown and the flesh is cooked through.

Carefully remove the fish from the pan and place it on a large serving dish. Sprinkle the crisp onions over the fish and garnish with the coriander and lemon wedge. Serve immediately.

400g/14oz pomfret
6 tbsp oil
1 small onion, finely sliced
A small handful of chopped fresh coriander
1 wedge lemon

For the spice paste:
1 onion, chopped
2 green chiles, chopped
1cm/$\frac{1}{2}$ in cube fresh ginger, peeled and finely chopped
10 curry leaves (optional)
10 black peppercorns
$\frac{1}{2}$ tsp chile powder
$\frac{1}{2}$ tsp turmeric powder
2 tbsp vinegar
1 tsp lemon juice
Salt

SERVES 2-4

CRAB CURRY

An unusual curry of crab cooked in its shell, this dish is a little bit messy to eat, but I believe this just adds to the enjoyment of the meal. In India, it is a very popular dish to serve during festivals, when the pieces of crab are presented to guests on banana leaves and they use their hands to prize the meat from the shell.

Heat the oil in a large frying pan and fry the onions for 5 minutes or until they are soft. Add the curry leaves, green chiles, garlic and ginger and cook for 5 minutes over a medium heat.

Add the chile and turmeric powders to the pan. Pour in 225ml/8floz of water, stirring slowly. Bring the mixture to the boil, then lower the heat and simmer for 10 minutes, stirring occasionally.

Add the crab pieces and continue cooking the curry over a medium heat for 10 minutes.

Stir in the coconut milk and allow the curry to heat through gently for 2 to 3 minutes. Add salt to taste. Remove the pan from the heat and set aside for a few minutes. Pour in the fresh lemon juice and serve immediately.

5 tbsp oil
2 red onions, finely sliced
20 curry leaves
4 green chiles
3 cloves garlic, chopped
2.5cm/1in cube fresh ginger, peeled and finely sliced
$\frac{1}{2}$ tsp chile powder
$\frac{1}{2}$ tsp turmeric powder
400g/14oz crab, cleaned and quartered
300ml/11floz fresh or canned coconut milk
1 tsp lemon juice
Salt

SERVES 4

ROAST KOONTHAL

In the coastal parts of Kerala, this is a very traditional and popular snack, often made by fishermen on their boats when they are out fishing. It is a dry dish that can be served before a meal, as an appetizer, in the same way that one would present olives to guests. Enjoy it with a glass of cold beer.

Clean the squid thoroughly. Cut it into 1cm/½ in pieces and set aside.

Heat the oil in a large frying pan. Add the onions and cook for 5 minutes or until they are golden brown.

Stir in the green chiles, ginger and curry leaves then add the chile powder and ground coriander. Mix well and add the tomatoes. Cook over a medium heat for 5 to 10 minutes, until the tomatoes break down to give a thick sauce.

Add the squid and mix thoroughly. Cover and continue cooking over a low heat for 15 minutes, stirring occasionally to prevent burning and sticking — if the dish becomes very dry too quickly, stir in a few spoonfuls of water. Remove from the heat and serve.

400g/14oz squid
5 tbsp oil
2 large onions, sliced
3 green chiles
2.5cm/1in cube fresh ginger, peeled and finely sliced
10 curry leaves
½ tsp chile powder
½ tsp ground coriander
2 large tomatoes, sliced

SERVES 4

PRAWN KEBAB

North Indians have a habit of always including milk products in a meal. Paneer cheese, a Punjabi delicacy, tends to be matched with everything, even other forms of protein. I was given this recipe by one of the chefs in our restaurants — it is typical of the new fusion style of Indian cooking, which can be quite a revelation. Indian people are increasingly bored with their traditional dishes and this type of recipe helps to regenerate interest.

To make the spice paste, place all the ingredients in a blender with 6 tablespoons of water and a little salt, and process to a fine paste.

Transfer the paste to a large bowl, add the yogurt and mix well. Stir in the prawns, the bell peppers and the onion and set aside to marinate for 1 hour.

Spear the prawns, vegetables and paneer alternately onto wooden or metal skewers.

Heat 4 tablespoons of the oil in a large frying pan. Place the kebabs in the pan and cook over a medium heat for 10 minutes, turning regularly so that they brown evenly.

In a separate frying pan, heat another 2 tablespoons of oil, then add the mustard seeds and curry leaves. As the mustard seeds begin to pop, pour the contents of the pan over the cooked kebabs.

Transfer the kebabs to serving plates and garnish them with the freshly grated coconut. Serve with salad and coconut chutney.

3 tbsp plain yogurt
450g/1lb large prawns
1/2 red bell pepper, seeded and cut into chunks
1/2 yellow bell pepper, seeded and cut into chunks
1/2 red onion, cut into small chunks
100g/3 1/2 oz paneer cheese, cubed
6 tbsp oil
1 tsp mustard seeds
A few curry leaves
20g/3/4oz freshly grated coconut
Salt

For the spice paste:
5 green chiles
3 red chiles
2 cloves garlic
2.5cm/1in cube fresh ginger, peeled and chopped
2 tbsp lemon juice
2 tbsp vinegar
1 tbsp cumin seeds
1 tbsp garam masala
A large pinch of turmeric powder

SERVES 4

CHEMMEN MANGA CURRY

Chemmen are shrimp and this dish is typical of the Cochin fishing community. As in so many fishing ports around the world, fishermen find shrimp hard to sell because everyone seems to want big prawns. This curry is therefore cheap to make, and is produced when mangoes are in season.

Heat the oil in a large saucepan. Add the mustard seeds and, as they begin to pop, add the onions, green chile, ginger and curry leaves. Cook over a medium heat for 5 to 7 minutes or until the onions are brown. Add the chile powder and turmeric, mix well and sauté for another 2 minutes.

Stir in 225ml/8floz of water and bring the mixture to the boil. Lower the heat and cook for 5 minutes. Add the shrimp and mangoes, then raise the heat to medium and continue cooking for another 5 minutes, stirring occasionally.

Lower the heat under the pan, add the coconut milk and simmer for a further 5 minutes, stirring constantly, until the sauce thickens and the prawns are well cooked. Add salt to taste and serve hot.

2 tbsp oil
1 tsp mustard seeds
2 onions, finely sliced
2 green chiles, sliced
2.5cm/1in cube fresh ginger, peeled and sliced
A few curry leaves
1 tsp chile powder
1 tsp turmeric powder
450g/1lb shrimp
2 small green mangoes, peeled and chopped
200ml/7floz fresh or canned coconut milk
Salt

SERVES 4

desserts & drinks

134 desserts & drinks

KERALA FRUIT SALAD

This is not a traditional dish — in Kerala we tend to eat fruit plain — but it is a very popular dessert in our restaurants, where it offers a refreshing end to a meal. One of the attractions is the variety of tropical fruit it includes. The sauce began as an experiment of mine; it combines Kerala's cashews with almonds and pistachios from North India.

Place the ingredients for the sauce into a blender and process for 2 to 3 minutes or until smooth.

Transfer the mixture to a small saucepan and heat for 5 to 7 minutes over a medium heat, stirring slowly. Remove from the heat and set aside.

To make the fruit salad, place the prepared fruit in a large bowl and pour over the lime juice. Mix well, then either pour the sauce over the fruit straight away, or serve the fruit in individual dishes and top with the sauce just before serving. Garnish with chopped nuts if desired.

For the sauce:
50g/2oz raw cashew nuts
50g/2oz raw almonds
50g/2oz raw pistachio nuts
75g/3oz white sugar
100ml/3½ floz single cream

For the fruit salad:
1 mango, peeled and diced
½ pineapple, peeled and diced
2 bananas, peeled and finely sliced
2 apples, peeled and diced
2 cheekoo, peeled and finely sliced
1 kiwi fruit, peeled and finely sliced
1 small guava, peeled and diced
A few grapes, halved
Seeds and flesh of 1 passion fruit
Juice of 1 lime
2 tbsp chopped mixed nuts (optional)

SERVES 4

BANANA DOSA

When freshly cooked, these banana pancakes are delicious served plain, but for a more glamorous presentation at a dinner party, for example, try topping them with coconut ice cream. In Kerala they are made for auspicious occasions such as weddings, to provide a change from more everyday desserts such as milky rice puddings. These dosa are also popular in Brahmin homes.

In a large bowl, place the bananas, rice flour, plain flour, sugar, oil, cardamon and salt. Make a well in the centre and pour in 100ml/3½ floz of water. Blend with a wooden spoon to give a thick batter of dropping consistency, adding a little more water or flour if required.

Heat a frying pan over a medium heat. Rub the surface with some oil using a brush or kitchen paper. Pour a large spoonful of the batter into the pan and spread it out lightly. Cook for 5 minutes or until golden brown underneath, then turn over and cook for a further 3 minutes.

Remove the dosa and set aside in a warm place while you cook the remaining mixture. Serve hot, with ice cream if desired.

4 ripe bananas, peeled and mashed thoroughly
200g/7oz rice flour
100g/3½ oz plain flour
2 tbsp white sugar
2 tbsp oil, plus extra for greasing
A pinch of ground cardamon
A pinch of salt
4 scoops coconut ice cream, to serve (optional)

SERVES 4

COCONUT HALWA

Coconut is one of the main ingredients in South Indian cooking and we make a wide variety of puddings with it. This is one of the easiest.

In a small frying pan, heat 1 tablespoon of the ghee. Add the cashew nuts and cook for 2 to 3 minutes or until golden, then remove from the heat and drain on kitchen paper. Grease a baking tray with a little ghee and set aside.

Place the coconut in a blender and grind for 1 minute or until coarse, then set aside.

In a heavy saucepan, bring 450ml/16floz of water to the boil, add the sugar and cook over a medium heat for 10 minutes, stirring frequently until the sugar syrup is thick.

Add the coconut and the remaining 4 tablespoons of ghee and cook over a low heat, stirring constantly, until the ingredients are throughly combined and the mixture comes easily away from the side of the pan.

Add the fried cashew nuts and cardamon, stirring well. Spread the mixture onto the greased baking tray. Leave to cool, then chill for 4 hours or until set. Cut into pieces and serve cold.

5 tbsp ghee, plus extra for greasing
25g/1oz raw cashew nuts
200g/7oz freshly grated or desiccated coconut
400g/14oz white sugar
1 tsp ground cardamon

MAKES 15

KESARI

Using a pestle and mortar, crush the whole cardamon pods to a fine powder. Set aside.

Heat 1 tablespoon of the ghee in a frying pan over a medium heat. Add the cashew nuts and raisins and cook, stirring, until the cashews brown and the raisins swell. Remove from the heat, drain on kitchen paper and set aside.

Heat the milk, sugar and saffron in a heavy saucepan until the sugar dissolves. When the milk begins to boil, remove it from the heat and set aside.

In a large, heavy pan, melt $100g/3\frac{1}{2}oz$ of the ghee over a medium heat. Add the semolina, lower the heat and cook, stirring constantly, until brown.

Slowly add the flavoured milk to the semolina, stirring quickly. Mix in the remaining ghee, then the cashew nuts, raisins and cardamon. Stir until the mixture forms a thick paste; if necessary, add a little extra ghee until the semolina sticks together.

Serve warm straight from the pan, or transfer the mixture to a greased shallow tray and spread out, smoothing over the top. Leave to cool, then chill the mixture for about 4 hours or until set. To serve, cut into squares and top with a scoop of mango sorbet, if desired.

5 cardamon pods
200g/7oz ghee, plus extra
  for greasing
1 tbsp broken raw cashew
  nuts
1 tbsp raisins
400ml/14floz milk
150g/5oz white sugar
2-3 pinches saffron threads
200g/7oz semolina
500ml/18floz mango sorbet,
  to serve (optional)

MAKES 15

CARROT KHEER

Heat 2 tablespoons of the ghee in a small frying pan
and cook the cashews and raisins until the nuts are
golden brown. Remove from the heat and drain on
kitchen paper.

In a heavy saucepan, heat the remaining 3 tablespoons
of ghee over a medium heat. Add the grated carrot
and sauté for 5 minutes. Pour in the milk and sugar,
stirring well, then bring the mixture to the boil
and simmer for 10 minutes, stirring constantly,
until the carrot is well cooked.

Add the cardamon, fried cashews and raisins and cook
for a further 10 minutes, stirring constantly, until
the volume has reduced by half. Remove from the heat
and serve hot, sprinkled with a little more ground
cardamon if desired.

5 tbsp ghee
50g/2oz raw cashew nuts
50g/2oz raisins
250g/9oz carrots, grated
1.2 litres/2 pints milk
150g/5oz white sugar
1 tsp ground cardamon, plus
* extra for serving*

SERVES 4

PAL GOVA

Grease a large baking tray or flat dish with some ghee
and set aside. In a heavy saucepan, simmer the milk
for 15 minutes, stirring constantly. Add the sugar
and semolina and continue simmering for a further
10 minutes, stirring constantly.

When the milk has reduced by about half in volume,
lower the heat and slowly add the ghee a spoonful at
a time, stirring well after each addition. Continue
cooking and stirring for another 15 to 20 minutes or
until the mixture turns very thick and comes away
from the side of the pan. Mix in the cardamon.

Transfer the mixture to the greased tray and spread out
well with a spatula or round-bladed knife, smoothing
over the surface. Leave to cool, then place in the
fridge for 2 hours to set. Cut into small squares or
diamonds and serve cold.

125g/4$\frac{1}{2}$oz ghee, plus
* extra for greasing*
1.2 litres/2 pints milk
200g/7oz white sugar
100g/3$\frac{1}{2}$oz semolina
1 tsp ground cardamon

MAKES 15

ADA PRADHAMAN

If using adai or pudding rice, place it in a saucepan
    of boiling water and simmer for 15 minutes until
    tender but firm, then drain and set aside; if using
    flaked rice, you do not need to pre-cook it.

Place the coconut in a blender with 450ml/16floz of
    water and blend for 5 minutes. Strain the mixture
    through a muslin cloth or very fine sieve into a
    bowl, squeezing out as much of the water as you can.
    Set the liquid aside.

Transfer the coconut solids to a separate bowl and add
    450ml/16floz of water. Stir well and filter again
    into another bowl. Add another 225ml/8floz of water
    to the second bowl and stir well. Keep the bowls of
    coconut milk separate.

In a small frying pan, heat 2 tablespoons of the ghee.
    Add the cashew nuts and raisins and cook, stirring,
    until the cashews turn golden brown. Remove from the
    pan, drain on kitchen paper and set aside.

In a heavy saucepan, bring 225ml/8floz of water to the
    boil and add the jaggery or brown sugar. Reduce the
    heat to medium and stir with a wooden spoon until
    the sugar dissolves. Return to the boil and simmer
    for 5 minutes to give a thick syrup.

Lower the heat again and add the adai, rice or rice
    flakes. Cook for a further 10 minutes over a low
    heat, stirring frequently.

When most of the liquid has been absorbed, add the
    remaining ghee a spoonful at a time, mixing well.

Add the most dilute bowl of coconut milk to the pan
    and cook for 5 minutes, stirring. Then add the more
    concentrated bowl of coconut milk, plus the cashews
    and raisins. Mix well and remove from the heat. Keep
    stirring for 2 to 3 minutes away from the heat then
    serve hot, or leave to cool before serving.

*250g/9oz adai, pudding
    rice or rice flakes*
*300g/10½ oz freshly
    grated or desiccated
    coconut*
6 tbsp ghee
50g/2oz raw cashew nuts
50g/2oz raisins
*200g/7oz jaggery or brown
    sugar*

SERVES 4

PAL PAYASAM

This is Kerala's version of rice pudding, spiced with cardamon and enriched with ghee, cashews and raisins. It is a simple everyday dessert, unlike ada pradhaman which, although equally famous, is not often made in homes because its preparation is time-consuming. Be very careful when heating the milk and cooking the rice as milk can burn easily: stir the mixture continuously and adjust the heat to suit your saucepan.

Using a pestle and mortar, crush the whole cardamon pods to a fine powder. Set aside.

Heat the ghee in a heavy frying pan and sauté the cashews and raisins together until the cashews are golden and the raisins swell up. Drain on kitchen paper and set aside.

Wash and drain the rice. In a large, heavy saucepan, heat the milk for 10 minutes, stirring constantly. Add the rice and continue to stir over a medium heat until the rice is nearly cooked.

Add the sugar and continue to stir until the sugar has dissolved and the rice is well cooked. Stir in the cashews, raisins and cardamon powder and serve hot.

7-8 cardamon pods
2 tbsp ghee
2 tbsp broken raw cashew nuts
2 tbsp raisins
100g/3$\frac{1}{2}$ oz basmati rice
600ml/1 pint milk
100g/3$\frac{1}{2}$ oz white sugar

SERVES 4

KOZHUKATTA

My mother's special recipe: she makes this for the Onam festival when the whole family gets together. The combination of coconut and jaggery is a particular favourite with children but here it is made more interesting by being steamed inside a light rice flour batter.

Place the rice flour and a little salt in a large bowl. Make a well in the centre and slowly stir in 225ml/8floz of warm water. Add the oil and mix well to give a bread-like dough, adding more flour or water as necessary. Set aside.

To make the filling, melt the ghee in a large frying pan over a medium heat. Add the coconut, jaggery and cardamon and cook, stirring, over a low heat for 5 to 7 minutes, until the mixture is thick and the jaggery has dissolved. Set aside to cool.

Using greased hands, take a piece of dough about the size of a golfball and shape it into a flat patty. Place a small spoonful of the coconut mixture in the middle of the dough and fold the dough around it to completely seal in the filling. Gently roll it into a ball then set aside on a plate while you repeat the process with the remaining dough and filling.

Using a steamer or metal colander placed over a large saucepan of boiling water, steam the balls for 15 minutes until the dough is cooked through. Serve the kozhukatta hot or cold.

225g/8oz rice flour
1 tbsp vegetable oil
Salt

For the filling:
1 tbsp ghee
100g/3½oz freshly grated
  or desiccated coconut
50g/2oz jaggery or brown
  sugar, roughly chopped
½ tsp ground cardamon

MAKES 12

LIME AND SODA

Pour the lime juice into a jug. Add the salt or sugar to taste, then add half the soda water and whisk until the salt or sugar is dissolved.

Add the rest of the water, stir and pour into serving glasses. Sprinkle a few cumin seeds and crushed chiles on top, if desired, before serving.

Juice of 4 limes
725ml/1 pint 5floz soda water
Salt or white sugar
Crushed cumin seeds
  (optional)
Crushed chiles (optional)

SERVES 4

BANANA LASSI

Place all the ingredients in a blender and process for 2 minutes. Pour the lassi into individual glasses and serve, or cover and store in the fridge for up to 24 hours.

250g/9oz plain yogurt
200g/7oz fresh peeled
  banana, cut into chunks
125ml/4floz milk
4 teaspoons white sugar,
  or to taste

SERVES 4

MORUM VELLAM

Place all the ingredients in a blender, adding salt to taste. Pour in 300ml/10$\frac{1}{2}$floz of water and process for 5 minutes or until very smooth.

Strain the mixture through a very fine sieve and serve cold, with crushed ice if desired.

300ml/10$\frac{1}{2}$ floz plain
  yogurt
2.5cm/1in cube fresh
  ginger, peeled and
  sliced
2 green chiles, chopped
A few curry leaves
Crushed ice, to serve
  (optional)
Salt

SERVES 2

cheekoo shake & banana chips

CHEEKOO SHAKE

Peel the fruit and chop the flesh roughly, removing all
the stones. Place in a blender with the milk and
sugar and process for 2 minutes. Add the crushed ice
and blend for a further 30 seconds.

Pour the liquid into individual glasses, sprinkle with
cardamon and serve immediately.

2 cheekoo
400ml/14floz milk
4 tsp white sugar
6 tbsp crushed ice
1 tsp ground cardamon

SERVES 4

MASALA TEA

You can use Assam teabags or loose leaf tea to make this drink. The spice
mixture can be kept in an airtight container for up to 1 month and used as
required. I recommend that you use ½ teaspoon of the spice mixture for every
cup of tea, but you can adjust the quantity to suit your taste.

To make the spice mixture, combine all the ingredients
in an airtight container and stir well.

To make the tea, place the milk and tea in a saucepan
with 250ml/9floz of water. Bring to the boil, add
1 teaspoon of the spice mixture and simmer for
5 minutes, stirring gently.

Remove from the heat and strain into cups using a very
fine sieve. Add sugar to taste and serve very hot.

For the spice mixture:
2 tbsp ground nutmeg
2 tbsp ground black pepper
1 tbsp ground cinnamon
½ tbsp ground cardamon
1 tsp ground ginger
2 cloves, ground

For the tea:
2 tbsp Assam tea
250ml/9floz milk
White sugar

SERVES 2

MENU PLANNER

The following is a selection of traditional-style menus compiled from recipes in this book. In Kerala we would normally serve the food on banana leaves rather than ceramic plates and instead of cutlery we would use our hands.

MENU 1
starters
Masala vadai
Vegetable samosa
Coconut chutney

main course
Rasa koottu
Black-eye bean thoran
Thakkali choru
Uthappam

dessert
Ada pradhaman

MENU 2
starters
Chinnappam
Kathrikka
Banana boli
Coriander chutney

main course
Moru kachiathu with green
 banana & mango
Shallot curry
Nair dosa
Tamarind rice
Appam

dessert
Kesari

MENU 3
starters
Banana chips
Mango pickle
Roast koonthal

main course
Meen porichathu
Chicken green masala
Bhindi kichadi
Lemon rice
Ari pathiri

dessert
Kozhukatta

MENU 4
starters
Achappam
Cashew nut pakodas
Garlic pickle

main course
Attu varuval
Beet pachadi
Kadachakka stew
Potato curry
Pilau rice
Uzhunnappam

dessert
Pal payasam

MENU 5
starters
Achappam
Kathrikka
Coriander chutney
Roast koonthal

main course
Meen pappas
Crab curry
Nadan parippu curry
Bhindi kichadi
Coconut rice
Appam

dessert
Banana dosa

FEAST MENU
starters
Achappam
Masala vadai
Banana boli
Lemon pickle

main course
Nair dosa
Crab curry
Shallot curry
Lemon rice
Uzhunnappam

dessert
Ada pradhaman

Indian food is now popular with people all round the world and this selection of contemporary menus shows how easily the dishes in this book can fit into everyday life. These recipes are all quick to make and the ingredients are readily available.

SUMMER MENU
starters
Kathrikka
Gooseberry pickle
Sundal
Morum vellam

main course
Prawn kebab
Moru kachiathu with
  green banana & mango
Green mango & shallot salad
Pilau rice
Uzhunappam

dessert
Kerala fruit salad

WINTER MENU
starters
Chinnappam
Cashew nut pakodas
Garlic pickle
Rasam

main course
Beef chile
Pepper masala
Tamarind rice
Poories

dessert
Pal payasam

LIGHT & HEALTHY DINNER
starters
Semolina uppuma
Coriander chutney
Cheekoo shake

main course
Tindori thoran
Bhindi kichadi
Coconut rice
Ari pathiri

dessert
Kerala fruit salad

VEGAN DINNER PARTY
starters
Banana boli
Sundal
Lemon pickle

main course
Brinjal curry
Drumstick thoran
Lemon rice

dessert
Banana dosa

BRUNCH
Cashew nut pakoda
Coconut chutney
Motta roast
Uthappam
Masala tea

QUICK LUNCHES
Kathrikka
Thakkali curry
Lemon rice
Banana lassi

Sundal
Moru kachiathu with
  green banana & mango

Pilau rice
Guava salad
Green pea masala
Ari pathiri

QUICK SUPPERS
Pepper chicken
Nadan parippu curry
Wheat dosa

Kozhy mappas
Green pea masala
Lemon rice

Corn ohaji
Spinach bhaji
Poories

GLOSSARY

Adai: or rice chips are made from rice flour batter that is spread on banana leaves, folded and dropped into boiling water. Once the batter is cooked, the banana leaf is removed from the water and allowed to cool. It is then opened to reveal the cooked rice paste, which is left to dry and finally broken into pieces. If you cannot find adai in Indian shops, use flaked or pudding rice instead.

Bhindi: also known as okra or ladies' fingers, this tapered green vegetable is highly favoured in Indian restaurants. It can take on a slimy texture when cooked for long periods but in South Indian thorans, for example, it is stir-fried to maintain its crunchy texture. Bhindi can be bought fresh or frozen in supermarkets.

Breadfruit: a large round fruit with a spiky skin, this is also known as kadachakka and commonly found in tropical countries. Inside, the fruit is pale and, when cooked, has a texture almost like that of well-cooked aubergine. Breadfruit is not very absorbent and so is not receptive to heavy spicing.

Chat Masala: a spice mix frequently used to flavour snack preparations in North and West India. It is a combination of white and black salt with, amongst other things, chile, ginger and dried mango. Its salty and yet sweet flavour makes it particularly good in fresh salads and with yogurt. It tends to be on sale only in specialist shops.

Cheekoo: a fruit that externally resembles a potato or kiwi and has a flavour somewhere between a pear and a fig. Discard the skin and seeds before enjoying the soft brown flesh. In India this rich fruit is believed to be good for the circulation.

Coconut: the fruit of a palm tree that grows in abundance in Kerala. Although brown, hairy and rather unsightly on the outside, the inside surprises with sweet, refreshing water and deliciously crunchy white flesh. Coconut is essential to South Indian cooking and is revered by Indian people as the fruit of the gods. It enhances any dish, sweet or savoury. To my mind, there is something sublime about its sweet, nutty flesh.

Curry Leaves: used as a herb, these are the leaves of the kariveppu tree, which grows to around two metres tall and is commonly found in South India. When fried, the leaves have a nutty flavour and pleasing crispness. In India it is believed they are good for hair growth. Curry leaves, which are used frequently in this book, are readily available in specialist Asian shops and are increasingly available in regular supermarkets.

Drumstick: an appropriate name for a long, thin vegetable with a woody skin. It grows on a seven-metre high tree, the long drumsticks hanging from the branches. Once cooked, the fibrous outer layer should be discarded before you enjoy the fleshy centre.

Ghee: this Asian clarified butter is very popular in the north of India however it is not used often in South Indian cooking. Puddings and sweets are the exception, and occasionally we stir it into rice.

Jaggery: a coarse, dark, unrefined sugar made from the dehydrated juice of crushed sugar cane. It has a unique sticky yet crumbly consistency and a distinctive musky flavour that is very different to that of regular granulated sugar. Not to be confused with the syrupy palm sugar of Southeast Asian cooking, jaggery can be replaced by brown or demerara sugar in the recipes in this book, but really there is no substitute for it.

Mango: a symbol of plenty in India, where the mango season is eagerly awaited. Green unripened mangoes of any variety are used in curries and to make pickles. They can be peeled, however the skin adds a distinctive and delicious flavour.

Mustard seeds: those referred to in these recipes are the brown variety, which can be found in most supermarkets. South Indians believe that when the seeds pop during cooking they release a special aroma that tempts guests. Mustard seeds also lend a delicious flavour to recipes and are frequently combined with curry leaves and sometimes dried chiles. The recipes will work without them, but mustard seeds do add a touch of magic.

Oil: where oil is specified in this book it refers to vegetable oil. In South India we tend to use both vegetable oil and coconut oil when cooking. Coconut oil has an amazing flavour but it is high in saturated fat, which is a health concern to many people. In general, the use of any oil in our style of cooking is kept to a minimum.

Papaya: a large tropical fruit with small black seeds and rich orange flesh. In Indian cooking the fruit is used as a vegetable in curries when it is green and unripe; when ripe and golden it is used in fruit salads and squeezed to make a delicious drink.

Plantain: rather like an over-sized banana, but with a thicker skin and starchier flesh, plantain is widely used in South Indian cooking. About nine different types of plantain are grown in Kerala. When green, or unripe, they are used in curries as a vegetable; when ripe they are steamed and eaten for breakfast.

Rice: regular long-grain rice is most common in India and to my mind is the best for everyday eating. It is good value for money and filling (key attractions to Indian people) although it does not have the fragrance of the more expensive basmati variety. Where basmati is specified in this book, it is certainly the best choice, however most of the recipes use long-grain.

Tamarind: a sweet-sour fruit encased in a pod and found growing on trees in tropical regions. When unripe the pod is green; as it dries out and turns brown, the fruit inside ripens and turns a chocolate colour. In India tamarind is sun-dried with salt and can be kept for months. Frequently used in curries, it is sold in many supermarkets, either as a liquid concentrate or in a compressed block of pulp.

Tindori: a vegetable that can be obtained in most Asian shops, and you may occasionally come across it in supermarkets. Also known as kovakka, they look like miniature cucumbers but have a smooth and shiny skin that is lightly flecked with yellow. Their crunchy texture is perfect for thoran.

Urad dal: dal is the Indian word for lentils or pulses. Urad dal is a black lentil that is sold either whole, split, or skinned and split. The latter is the one I refer to in this book. In South India it is used to add a nutty flavour and chewy texture to thorans, or ground and made into dosas. In North Indian cookery, whole urad dal are more commonly used.

Yogurt: one of the main souring agents in South Indian cooking. In dishes such as Moru kachiathu there is a wonderful tension between the sweet mango and the tangy sourness of the yogurt sauce. Remember to allow hot dishes to cool slightly before adding yogurt, otherwise it will curdle.

RECIPE INDEX

ACKNOWLEDGMENTS

My wife Alison has been the greatest source of inspiration for me to write and finish this book in the middle of our busy lives running the three Rasa restaurants. Mum and Dad gave me the best possible advice over the telephone and on our occasional meetings in Kerala. I have drawn on everything I learned from them as a child at home and at Dad's tea shop. I would like to thank Jenni Muir for her valuable support and hard work. Also my team of excellent chefs: Narayan, Pramod, Madhu, Binu and Rajan for their help in the seafood and meat sections of the book. May I also thank Susie, David Loftus and Vanessa for their creative work on the pictures and Elaine Collins and Lucy Alexander for their contributions to the project.

Conran Octopus would like to thank the following organisation for their kind permission to reproduce photographs in this book: page 8 Maja Koene/Colorific Photo Library Ltd.